DAVID BOOTH / JENNIFER ROWSELL

THE
LITERACY PRINCIPAL

Leading, supporting and assessing reading and writing initiatives

Foreword by Michael Fullan

WITHDRAWN

Pembroke Publishers Limited

To

Jay and Katie

Madeleine and Fred

© 2002 **Pembroke Publishers**
538 Hood Road
Markham, Ontario, Canada L3R 3K9
www.pembrokepublishers.com

Distributed in the U.S. by Stenhouse Publishers
477 Congress Street
Portland, ME 04101
www.stenhouse.com

We acknowledge the financial support of the Government of Canada through the Book Publishing Industry Development Program (BPIDP) for our publishing activities.

National Library of Canada Cataloguing in Publication

Booth, David W. (David Wallace)
    The literacy principal : leading, supporting and assessing reading and writing initiatives / David Booth, Jennifer Rowsell ; foreword by Michael Fullan.

Includes bibliographical references and index.
ISBN 1-55138-146-X

    1. Reading. 2. English language—Rhetoric—Study and teaching.
I. Rowsell, Jennifer. II. Title.

LB1576.B68 2002   428.4'071   C2002-902917-1

Editor: Jennifer Drope
Cover Design: John Zehethofer
Typesetting: JayTee Graphics

Printed and bound in Canada
9 8 7 6 5 4 3 2

Contents

Foreword

The subjective world of principals is such that many of them suffer from the same problem in "implementing a new role as facilitator of change" as do teachers in implementing new teaching roles: What the principal should do specifically to manage change at the school level is a complex affair for which the principal has little preparation. The psychological and sociological problems of change that confront the principal are at least as great as those that confront teachers. Without this sociological sympathy, many principals will feel exactly as teachers do. Other people simply do not seem to understand the problems they face.

From *The New Meaning of Educational Change*
by Michael Fullan

There are two types of expertise needed in order to seriously improve literacy in schools: one area is expertise in the *content* of literacy; the other is expertise in leading the *change process.*

Advancement in the effective content of teaching literacy has been marred by the fruitless, dichotomous debate of whole language versus phonics. Thankfully, we can put this debate behind us once and for all. In this book, David Booth and Jennifer Rowsell lay out all the elements of a comprehensive, balanced literacy program — cueing systems, stages of reading, literacy across the curriculum, assessment of literacy — all are carefully and fully treated as the authors consider how to design and monitor effective literacy programs.

Expertise in leading the change process involves an entirely different set of knowledge and skills — different in the sense that one can be an expert in literacy, but a disastrous change agent at the same time. Literacy education, like any innovation, requires change leadership. As the authors make clear and illustrate through description and vignettes, effective literacy implementation requires (among other change matters): principal leadership, principals as instructional leaders, a strong professional community, time for change, in-school professional development, district professional development, support for teachers, program focus, and support of parents and the community.

The strength of this book lies in the delineating and bringing together of these two sets of expertise. All school districts and state systems are currently focusing on the fundamentals of literacy. *The Literacy Principal* is essential to guiding these efforts. It is a handbook that provides leaders with the basics of literacy programs, as well as the change leadership that must be integrated in school and district settings. As such, it is a rich and unique resource for all leaders who are committed to designing and establishing effective literacy programs across all schools.

Michael Fullan, Dean,
Ontario Institute for Studies in Education,
University of Toronto

Introduction: Leading from Within

... We managed to have a track team, a school band, a student newspaper, a parent-teacher association, a committee of concerned parents, a karate class, and an adult education evening program. I have outlived two teachers' strikes, three students' rebellions and one community riot. ...

Handling teachers requires much tact. Mr. Cohen regularly threatens to leave. He is not the most diplomatic person I've ever met, yet, mysteriously, the highest percentage of good readers come out of Cohen's class. Mr. Nigeria Green is definitely a black nationalist problem. It is all I can do to restrain him from painting his classroom walls black, red and green. According to him, black for our color, green for the land to which we must return, and red for the blood which must be spilled to obtain it. He has fewer dropouts and less absenteeism than any other class, the highest library attendance, and his boys are the backbone of our track team. Bernard Cohen and Nigeria Green do not get along very well, but the kids fare a bit better because they're both here.

Excerpt from *A Hero Ain't Nothin' but a Sandwich*

This principal's words reflect a reality of leadership today — running schools has become a complicated business. They also imply another fact — literacy stands at the forefront of the important concerns on a leader's agenda, with the presiding question being: How should schools be organized so that teachers can help children to develop as proficient readers and writers?

Educators face several challenges at once: test scores rise and fall; school results are compared; the literacy difficulties of certain groups of students increase; technology swallows the budgets for books; class sizes increase; parent demands become more strident; and resources for special-needs children shrink. Yet, despite the challenges, there are many teachers, schools and districts pioneering new literacy programs based on solid research, and their successes offer other school communities inspiration as they rethink and develop their own plans for implementing an effective reading and writing curriculum for all students.

These individual, schoolwide and district-based initiatives are the basis of this book, as we examine the teaching of literacy, both in theory and in practice. Our goal is to offer support to school leaders as they journey into literacy-based school change. Quick fixes like adopting a miraculous published program, or instituting another set of tests will not, on their own, cause children to become literate. However, there are ways of creating school communities where literacy is the bedrock of the curriculum—where children recognize it as necessary and integral to their participation in authentic language activities and events that require thoughtful and mindful reading and writing. But how is this achieved?

Although it is easier to describe than accomplish, there are some guiding principles for school leaders that can form a framework for literacy-based school change:

- Create a school literacy team that has a shared vision of what is possible and even achievable. This will help prepare the members of the team for the difficult times when they may need to modify and even alter plans for implementing literacy initiatives.
- Encourage everyone to participate collaboratively in the process. Administrators, teachers, students, parents and support staff need to forge a common understanding about the goals they hope to achieve.
- Work together as a team to examine teaching practices, explore new ideas, set priorities, establish shared goals, decide on tasks and determine who will complete them.
- Ensure that all members of the team are stakeholders in the success of literacy initiatives, and that they receive credit for their efforts. A collective effort to create literacy-based school change is far more effective than a leader imposing his or her ideas on the staff.

Research in the theory and practice of literacy teaching is ongoing, and school leaders need to establish new reasons and new ways to examine programs so that everyone can continue to grow professionally. One way to achieve this is to empower others to make decisions. As Paul Shaw points out in his article *The Principal's Role*:

If you want teachers to become empowered then you have to trust them to make decisions wisely, to spend their money wisely, to communicate with parents wisely. The fascinating thing is that when teachers take control they become more committed, they work harder, they become more knowledgeable; when they take part in sustained, focused dialogue, they become more confident with parents, who in turn become more convinced that our school is doing a good job; when teachers begin to articulate their view of the children's learning and their view of their own learning and see parallels, the control is moving from the office to the teachers, from the teachers to the students.

In seeking to create a literate school community, all members of a school's literacy team need to become researchers, making use of their own experiences, as well as information in reports, professional articles and books, to gather data that can be analyzed. Making decisions about literacy initiatives then rests on interpreting the data in the context of a particular situation—the quicker everyone is in participating in this research process, the sooner the school can move into an action plan.

Challenging personal assumptions is the hallmark of inquiry, and research data on literacy can assist members in coming to terms with where change needs to take place within the school. This process is recursive, and participants need to share their experiences through reflection and discussion as they revalue and reconsider the literacy initiatives they have taken on.

It is important to remember that our end goal is to have every child in a school develop as a literate human being. For teachers, literacy instruction is a complex and at times onerous task, with students at many different stages of reading and writing development. To become more literate, children need to see themselves, their classmates, their teachers and their administrators as members of a literate community. Children in literacy difficulty especially need to experience what successful literacy events feel like, be recognized for their successes in the processes of reading and writing, and have their accomplishments celebrated.

By learning to make choices in their literacy lives, children begin to take ownership of not only what they read and write (e.g., fiction, information, poetry), but also the manner in which they read or write it (e.g., in groups, silently on their own, at home with a parent). They need to be supported not only by their teachers and their parents in their struggles toward independence, but by the school principal as well. To acknowledge the multiplicity of literacy needs in a school brings a principal that much closer to achieving targets or meeting action plans for literacy initiatives.

In defining the role of leadership in literacy-based school change, it is important to unite both the theory and the practice from two burgeoning fields: literacy teaching/learning and school change. As Michael Fullan so aptly sets the stage in the Foreword, new research in the field of literacy cannot be separated from the changing face of leadership.

We see this book as a series of conversations — between the two of us as authors, among the principals and administrators who shared with us their wise words during our interviews, and among the writers and researchers whose work stimulated our discourse. We have referenced the authorities that we used as a support to our work in the bibliography and we have annotated some seminal works at the end of each chapter that can offer you key principles for implementing literacy-based school change. Given our conversational writing style throughout the book, we have opted for more of an informal approach to citations from authorities in the field and interviewees by eliminating dates of publication and page numbers within the text itself.

In writing this book, we have tried to place literacy-based school change *within* literacy teaching to privilege children's development as readers and writers above all else. Designed to interweave the theoretical with the practical, each chapter explores a different aspect of the knowledge and skills necessary for becoming more effective literacy principals.

Chapter One begins by describing the five main categories of change factors required to embark on the process of creating literacy-based change in your school. Chapter Two outlines the literacy principles and practices that are essential to consider in supporting or leading literacy initiatives. Building from the first two chapters, Chapter Three then offers a comprehensive array of strategies for improving literacy at all levels—from individual students, to classrooms, the school and the school district. Finally, Chapter Four examines the need for a strong assessment and evaluation component in monitoring literacy, and provides a variety of modes to consider.

An added feature in the book is a professional development section at the end of each chapter with questions for reflection and suggested readings to act as a support as you pave the way for change. Each chapter also features the voice of a present or former principal in interview clips about his or her experience with literacy-based school change. Finally, interspersed throughout all chapters are snapshots of inspiring literacy principals.

CHAPTER ONE

Changing the Face of Literacy Education in Schools

Effective literacy teachers operate from a needs basis, yet they also must have a strong sense of what other supports would help them, so that they can draw on that and feed that into their practice. They can then use their professional knowledge and practice base to help guide what might be helpful in their literacy teaching at any point in the day.

Carol Rolheiser, Associate Dean, Ontario Institute for Studies in Education, University of Toronto

There are mounting pressures and expectations for schools to ensure that *all* students are acquiring the literacy skills they need to succeed in the future. As urban centers expand and immigration increases, there are growing numbers of students who are new to the country and who speak English as a second language. As a result, teachers are more beholden than ever before to provide literacy instruction that sets the groundwork for successful futures for our children. Unfortunately, support networks required to develop students' skills may not always be in place.

With the vast amount of theory and research available in the area of literacy and language development, there is certainly no lack of information, resources and materials in place to ensure success for all. Yet, sometimes schools still fall short of set standards and often fail to meet struggling students' needs for intensive literacy teaching. At the same time, school districts grapple with how to channel their mandate to improve students' literacy rates into a solid, unified and thorough vision with practical classroom strategies to implement such a vision. Ultimately, districts are limited by the amount of time, staff and resources they have at their disposal.

It is precisely for these reasons that districts and governments have committed to "literacy for all" as a key goal for their schools. With "literacy for all" as a district-wide mandate, it is necessary for teachers, school leaders, and district and government officials to allot more time in the curriculum for literacy development *and* to have more access to best practice examples of excellence in literacy teaching. What this entails is a greater understanding of what creates literacy-based school change, or more specifically, what creates changes in literacy standards and practices on the part of educational stakeholders. To achieve this, it is imperative that districts have access to research and information about the experience of other schools and other districts undertaking to improve their teaching of literacy.

As it stands, there is little research exploring the context of literacy-based school change. According to three recent field-based research reports, with Carol Rolheiser, the associate dean of OISE/UT, as the lead writer of the research teams: *There has been little exploration of the challenges and accelerators facing schools and districts as they attempt to improve their teaching of literacy. At the moment, there is a void in the literature vis-à-vis how schools are working toward creating improvements in literacy teaching and learning.*

Rolheiser and her teams, therefore, have identified these five categories of change factors as fundamental and foundational to literacy-based school change:

- Principal leadership
- Teachers' knowledge, skills and dispositions
- Professional community
- Program coherence
- Technical resources

Some of the issues at the heart of literacy-driven school change appear to be: How can schools change their infrastructure and classroom programs to improve student literacy achievement? With a strong literacy initiative in place, how can schools move forward? What can school leaders and their literacy teams do to bring about such changes?

Researchers and scholars clearly identify the important role of early literacy in the lives of children. Of all subject areas, literacy stands as one of the most effective vehicles for school change, in that success in literacy ensures success in other curriculum areas. That is, if students can read, write and talk effectively, they can participate more fully in other areas of learning.

Research shows that intensive early literacy initiatives in schools and districts result in higher levels of achievement in all areas of the curriculum. Alongside higher achievement levels in other subject areas, literacy initiatives create a greater nexus between home and school. Part and parcel of early literacy programs and initiatives is involving parents in their children's literacy development by having them read to their children at home and build environments conducive to literacy success.

Studies on school change demonstrate that although system-wide changes in policy and programs are important for large-scale change to occur, building the capacity for change in individual schools is essential to effective school reform. As Rolheiser explains: *Where schools have built teachers' knowledge, skills and dispositions, where they have created a professional community, where the programs have coherence and focus, where teachers' work is supported by appropriate resources, and where the leadership exists to both lead and support the work of the school, there we find improvements in school achievement.*

This is quite a list of demands, but when we create a school culture that believes in a professional community, that has a strong, coherent vision, that spends money on useful resources, and above all else, that constructs a leadership team standing behind a literacy-based school, we build the groundwork for effective literacy initiatives.

The Leadership Role

In the Foreword, Michael Fullan refers to leadership as the driving force behind change taking place in schools, and our discussion of literacy-based school change pivots on leadership. If there is one message we wish to send out it is that shifts in literacy teaching and learning have less to do with new information about literacy and much more to do with changes in the infrastructure of schools.

We have already touched on the central role of the principal as a lead voice in literacy initiatives. Schools that have successful literacy programs show evidence of strong principal leadership, with focused attention on setting a literacy agenda, supporting teachers, accessing resources and building a capacity for further growth.

Principals often plan, launch and monitor the creation of a school vision and explicitly or implicitly establish a school culture by encouraging collaborative efforts among colleagues, facilitating professional development and focusing on school strategies to improve standards. As will be discussed in more detail shortly, leadership tends to flourish when it is shared. While the principal choreographs shared leadership, it is important to acknowledge and encourage individuals in leadership positions within the school.

Principals as Instructional Leaders

To effectively plan, launch and monitor a literacy initiative or support others in this endeavor, principals need both an interest in and even a passion for literacy, alongside a knowledge base about literacy and language development. Like teachers, principals increasingly wear a number of hats. There is no doubt that this multitude of roles can pull a school leader away from an instructional framework and more into administrative duties and management tasks.

However, programs and initiatives that assist principals in generating and maintaining teacher enthusiasm for improving literacy instruction are essential elements of school literacy improvement. Therefore, principals need to enrich their own understanding of exemplary teaching strategies, materials, and assessment and evaluation techniques.

Snapshot of a Literacy Principal

Shelley Harwayne enjoyed acting as a substitute teacher in her school, when, for example, a teacher wanted to attend a professional development session. She was always prepared with a read-aloud selection from her own collection. She believes that principals are teachers and that literacy is a significant part of that role.

Principals as Supporters of Teachers' Needs

Principals who believe in and even feel passionately about a project or initiative, infuse momentum and purpose into its goals. Clear communication about project goals, literacy plans and policies, and professional development events helps keep everyone on track. Communicating goals to the group compels individual teachers and teaching teams to maintain a commitment to literacy initiatives and to improve literacy standards in a school.

Efforts to encourage a commitment to literacy initiatives are most effective when accompanied by genuine interest in supporting teachers' needs. To imbue collegiality and collaboration in his school, principal Steven Reid, who is featured in Leadership Voices in Chapter Three, describes how he tries to sit down with each teacher to discuss individual needs and how to mediate these needs with school goals: *We talked to teachers and grade team teachers, inviting them in one by one, to discover their strengths, what was needed as professional development and where they saw themselves in the school in the future. We also revisited school plans, so that we would be able to identify where our needs were and where we could set appropriate goals and targets. The board has targets that offer models: we considered our population of students and then set goals to meet those boardwide targets, over time.* The act of negotiating district-wide demands with teacher needs is a skill principals need to hone in order to effectively lead a literacy initiative.

Shared Leadership

Principals who share the responsibility of leadership are much more successful at creating positive change for teachers and students. The more evidence there is of teamwork in a school, the more significant the change in literacy standards.

Shared leadership builds an environment that supports planning time and collaboration and contributes to evenly parceling out leadership positions. The more leadership you give to teachers, the greater the teacher "buy-in" and commitment to a literacy project or initiative. As Carol Rolheiser notes, *This is of great value in times of leadership shortages as it serves to create a great cadre of teachers with leadership experiences within schools.*

A few models of shared leadership that have proven effective in supporting literacy-based school change are described below.

SCHOOL-BASED LEADERSHIP TEAMS

Some districts have developed a literacy support structure by creating leadership teams to build capacity at the school level. The effect of this model is greatly determined by the training team members receive in building a collaborative work culture dependent upon each school's context, so that they can sustain innovation and promote continuous improvement. Since the teams are largely composed of teachers, along with an administrator, the members need time to plan together to determine their course of action and to target specific improvements for their school. As well, these teams are strengthened by district support such as professional development sessions and summer institutes where they can be part of a network of educators, sharing information and strategies from the different schools involved in a literacy project.

TEACHER LEADERS

Some schools rely on teacher leaders in order to support literacy change. This model works in a school culture that is collegial and professional, and where teachers take responsibility for their own growth as educators and for changing the learning conditions in their school. It is necessary for those involved to be able to learn from other colleagues with similar status, in order to develop their expertise as a cohesive school community. Teacher leaders need to be able to understand the needs of and the varied competencies that different staff members bring to each of their classrooms, and to foster literacy change according to individual professional needs. Most important, teacher leaders need the support of their administration in working toward collaborative inquiry and professional growth.

LITERACY COORDINATOR

With some literacy initiatives, the administrative team comprises the principal as provider of support and mentorship and a literacy coordinator as a liaison with teaching staff and as a resident expert on literacy teaching and learning. With the Toronto District School Board's *Early Years Literacy Project,* for example, the literacy coordinator role is central to the planning, monitoring and implementing of literacy-based school change. The literacy coordinator not only organizes professional development sessions for staff, but also sets up and maintains a literacy resource room for teachers to visit when they need support in their literacy teaching. Literacy coordinators plan cooperatively with teachers and promote team work in meeting the targets of their school. In addition, literacy coordinators take on the following responsibilities:

- Assist teachers in developing and maintaining classroom materials
- Work closely with the *Reading Recovery*™ teacher
- Connect theory and classroom practice
- Coordinate data collection
- Mentor teachers by providing support, direction and assistance to meet individual needs
- Engage, influence and motivate staff to explore all areas of literacy
- Coordinate regular meetings to discuss progress on initiatives

Like teacher leaders, literacy coordinators drive change in schools by disseminating literacy information and inciting enthusiasm about improving students' reading and writing.

Teachers' Knowledge, Skills and Dispositions

In order to create literate schools, principals and administrative teams must ensure that teachers have the knowledge, skills and dispositions to not only choose effective teaching strategies or assessment strands, but more importantly, to have the wherewithal to do so. That teachers strongly benefit from building their knowledge, skills and dispositions, and that this has an impact on student achievement, has been proven time and time again. A teacher's professional knowledge is a key ingredient in a teacher's success with students.

What tends to be undermined in the triad of knowledge, skills and dispositions are the skills and dispositions required to effectively teach a core process like literacy. Building skills in lesson planning, in pedagogy, and in assessment and evaluation are as important as building dispositions to create change and higher expectations in students.

One of the more contentious areas in the field of literacy teaching is assessment and evaluation. Many of the schools implementing literacy initiatives differ in their approach to assessing reading and writing development. In Chapter Four we offer a compendium of assessment approaches, but in terms of creating a literacy-based environment, we want to highlight the kaleidoscope of possible perspectives one can take on instituting effective assessment and evaluation.

The School as a Strong Professional Community

Based on research and practice, successful schools have collaborative cultures in which administrators and teachers work as a team with a common commitment to literacy initiatives that ensure success for all. By creating a collaborative culture among educators on a literacy team, it is possible to incite interest in theory and new methodologies and practices in the area of literacy and language development. A collaborative culture naturally establishes partnerships with other possible team members, such as parents, in a common pursuit to improve literacy skills for all students.

It has been shown that if schools work as teams, there is much sharing of expertise so that all students benefit from the most effective literacy instruction available. To create a unified team committed to literacy-based school change, a school needs a specific, detailed and rigorous literacy plan that has a shared vision of how it will get from here to there. Literacy-driven schooling unites staff, parents and children by creating a culture of self-directed learning.

A collaborative culture provides a combination of pressure and support to help teachers deal with change and improve student learning. In *The New Meaning of Educational Change*, Michael Fullan describes this process as "the overlapping of strong pedagogical practice" married to the existence and implementation of assessment literacy. What is implicit in such a belief is that teachers need to work together with clear goals, while at the same time, with clear accountability. To move from a collaborative community to a professional community where teachers overlap strong pedagogy with assessment, teachers need the ability and desire to assess their students and to respond to the results of that assessment to inform their practice.

The students too need to be brought on board in creating successful literacy experiences. Paul Shaw envisions a school that believes in ranges and opportunities for choice across age groups. He points out that as children get older, their opportunities to choose diminish (i.e., the children who have the most choice are in kindergarten). With such a revelation in mind, educators need to reevaluate their images of the learner. Principals not only need to create collaborative school environments that promote professional development so that teachers can hone their practice, but also facilitate self-directed learning so that students at all grade levels have more choice in their learning. By taking control of their own learning, students become more independent, more in control, and ultimately make better choices in their learning.

What also lies at the heart of creating schools as professional communities is developing effective partnerships with parents. In Carol Rolheiser's studies, all of the schools involved in her teams' research spoke of the difficulties in engaging their communities. Admittedly, each school saw community involvement as vital to the success of literacy initiatives, but most encountered obstacles in consolidating an equal commitment from the community. Those schools that managed to overcome this resistance and actively engage parents in literacy initiatives gained immeasurably.

There are several factors that have proven instrumental in rejuvenating support for literacy initiatives and creating a strong professional community, including:

- Time for change
- In-school professional development
- District professional development
- Teacher motivation
- Support systems for teachers
- The support of parents

Time for Change

To create a culture of self-directed learning for both teachers and students, principals need to provide proper time and precious resources to allow all parties to thoroughly explore their needs and their interests in relation to literacy-based change. For teachers, time is a commodity. The reality in today's schools is that teachers often face 25 to 35 students during the day, and then spend time at the end of the day going over what happened in class and reflecting on student needs. There is rarely time in all of this to take part in formal professional development or to work alone or collaboratively on increasing knowledge and skills.

Paul Shaw provides some practical suggestions on how school leaders can carve out some teacher time for professional development. One suggestion he offers is that schools place professional development in the schedule and plan for a certain number of hours each year. He explains that providing time and space for professional development naturally creates a culture of change that is receptive to more inquiry and reflection.

Teachers need time both in-school and out-of-school to work alone or collaboratively on fields of interest, to discuss and share ideas with others, as well as to advance their knowledge and skills. Appreciating the background and experience that teachers bring to the classroom is part of the process of creating literacy-based change. Where principals have made time for change, the result is often a more dedicated staff—the key to the success of any initiative.

Snapshot of a Literacy Principal

Paul Shaw, with limited funds for professional development, organized a special session on teaching writing with Donald Graves by speaker phone. A committee of teachers orchestrated the session, organized the staff questions and led the entire successful event.

In-School Professional Development

Collaborative teaching and learning environments naturally infuse collegiality and cooperation with a desire for in-school professional development. Encouraging colleagues to pursue interests individually and to forge groups is part of a principal's job as the lead voice in literacy initiatives.

What distinguishes initiatives like the Toronto District School Board's *Early Years Literacy Project* or Great Britain's *National Literacy Hour* from other initiatives is the value they have placed on bringing teams of teachers together to create effective literacy-based school change. By working together to resolve challenges and issues around literacy teaching, teachers believe they can create partnerships and share practices. Welcoming, valuing and respecting the expertise and views of other educators—whether they are fellow teachers or administrators—maximizes the use of in-school knowledge and capacity. Likewise, creating an instructional focus within schools fosters an overall commitment to literacy projects.

A clear focus on in-school professional development in the field of literacy and language education is a must if literacy success for all is going to be addressed— not just for teachers, but for the administrator too. Steven Reid explains why it is essential for school principals to be learners themselves and model the importance of professional development: *People will often notice when I, as principal, spend time with literacy initiatives. Teachers, then, on the whole have a clearer understanding that I am willing to work with them in any way that I can.*

District Professional Development

In examining schools involved in major literacy initiatives, it is important to note that part of their success lies in the principals' support for off-site teacher professional development. Collaborative teams may be culled from across a district or entire schools may attend district-wide training sessions where grade teams have opportunities to voice specific issues, concerns, reflections and questions.

Exposure to such training creates a common language and a forum where staff members and other participants can voice their questions and concerns. In this way, district professional development facilitates built-in support from the district itself, as well as from teachers at other schools.

Principals and other literacy leaders, such as literacy coordinators, can also benefit greatly from bringing their strengths to the table at district-wide sessions, and then using or sharing the knowledge and skills gained back at their schools. As Carol Rolheiser observes: *The project moved them outside their own schools, to understand how others were seeing some of the problems, and to learn the strategies that others were using. For example, the principals delved into issues that they might worry about as administrators in their schools—things that may be more difficult to delegate. The literacy coordinators focused much more specifically on the content of literacy.*

Teacher Motivation

Teachers have an immense amount of work and, generally speaking, at times feel undervalued and underappreciated. Principals have to be aware of waning enthusiasm and, indeed, be mindful of not only building future success for their students, but also for their staff.

Part of building a successful future for teachers involves creating an incentive for them to build on their own teaching practice, thereby fostering improvement in student achievement. Time and professional development are two key pieces in the puzzle to increasing teachers' job professionalism and satisfaction. Imbuing enthusiasm for teaching and building in time to reflect on their own successes gives teachers more perspective on their own growth.

After some professional development and collaboration with colleagues, teachers usually begin to witness changes in their teaching practice and in their students' reading and writing achievement. These are landmark events, as they make much of the process seem tangible and thereby worthwhile. In studies on literacy-based school change, teachers mention that they are better teachers of literacy and that they are more aware of effective literacy-specific teaching strategies once they have witnessed successes in their classrooms.

Although literacy initiatives can add to teacher workload, they often demonstrate that time invested in development and growth in practice leads to more fulfillment and, to some extent, enjoyment in teaching because there are demonstrated results. The positive feedback and results derived from their new sets of skills have proven to motivate teachers.

As Kathryn Broad, a principal whose voice is featured in Chapter Two, notes: *Do you know, in your school, who the struggling readers are? Do you know who the successful readers and writers are? Do you know why? Do you know who the teachers are on your staff who are really successful teachers in literacy? Do you know how to forge networks that let that expertise be shared?* Asking and reflecting upon these types of questions leads the way to a school culture with literacy front and centre.

Support Systems for Teachers

There are a variety of ways that a principal can set up strong literacy-based support systems for teachers in a school. One way, as described earlier, is to appoint a literacy coordinator whose job it is to support teachers in implementing exemplary literacy programs.

A key ingredient in the success of major initiatives like the Toronto District School Board's *Early Years Literacy Project* and Great Britain's *National Literacy Hour* has been the role of a literacy coordinator as a resident authority and overall support to staff. With a literacy coordinator in place, teachers can benefit from a library of resources on offer, supplemental readings to clarify or add to a teacher's knowledge of key components of literacy teaching, useful teaching demonstrations, and, on the whole, a clearer instructional program.

In many cases, although teachers have the knowledge base and even access to resources for effective literacy programs, they do not always have the time to keep abreast of new trends or to update their libraries. With a literacy coordinator at hand, teachers have daily access to resources, are assisted in their classroom when the need arises, and have a resource person in place to enable them to work quickly on areas of their teaching that may need improvement.

The Support of Parents

For literacy teaching to be effective, there has to be both centripetal and centrifugal forces in which students' home literacy experiences are brought into the classroom and in-school literacy events and practices are taken back home. In short, the home-school nexus is vital to a successful project or initiative.

Involvement may take the form of parental participation in classroom or school events such as author days or literacy nights, as well as parental input at home by following up on reading and writing activities, and, of course, reading to children every day. Many teachers have commented on the fact that strategies for reading are easily shared with parents and that this enables them to give parents clear and simple techniques to use when reading with their children.

Several of the schools in one successful district-wide literacy project had literacy nights where parents become more informed about the goals of the project and listened to success stories. Literacy initiatives have also served as a bridge in communities in which many of the students' parents were learning English themselves and could benefit from programs in place at schools. In Steven Reid's school, the literacy team designed a program for at-risk readers in grades one, two and three. In this program, throughout the year, the staff phoned parents advising them of ideas for supporting literacy with their children and on where to get inexpensive reading materials to bring into their homes to support literacy with their children every day.

Program Coherence

Program coherence or consistency is key to effectively implementing a literacy initiative. Having said that, creating coherence in a large and diverse district is no easy task. Principals are given the unwieldy task of conciliating the multitudinous needs of teachers and students with policies mandated from the district or state/province. One of the ways to make the task manageable is to create coherence through a specific and detailed literacy plan. In addition, professional development, the cornerstone of any initiative, can be orchestrated by a literacy coordinator or members of a teaching staff.

With the increasing workload of teachers and the constant threat of policy fragmentation, principals and their staffs need to have a clear sense of how their own programs relate to the whole (i.e., how their school literacy policy matches policy mandates). However, this cannot be at the expense of meeting the needs of each micro-community — a literacy framework must have the latitude to accommodate the specific needs of individual staffs and students. Schools that have created goals based on the needs of their own school, as well as district and state/provincial mandates, have experienced a much smoother implementation curve. By creating coherence in an initiative, teachers gain a greater sense of how their goals fit into the overall goals of large-scale projects or initiatives.

Technical Resources

The provision of such technical resources as materials, time and money is an important factor in the building of literacy-based school change. It is not so much an issue of volume of resources as it is determining what the appropriate resources based on the needs of your school are. It is a matter of targeting needs and then finding resources that match those needs. Resources represent not only the materials that will be used, but also the professional development teachers will need to effectively teach literacy in their classrooms. Hence, time and money are as important as materials in implementing literacy initiatives.

Clearly, books are critical to literacy teaching, but the books that are chosen must match the needs of individual classes and students. This might be determined by such factors as whether a class has predominantly ESL students or whether there are more boys than girls in a classroom setting. It is particularly important to have a program in place that allows children to bring books home from school and perhaps have parents read to them.

Susan Schwartz, whose comments are featured in Chapter Four, highlights that an important part of a principal's job is ensuring that the teaching staff is equipped with what it needs to effectively teach literacy. This means taking account of macro-issues like program coherence and assessment, alongside micro-issues like keeping tabs on the availability of supplies. She emphasizes: *Resources are a large part of teaching, and teachers need to know that their resources are there for their programs.*

Snapshot of a Literacy Principal

As a secondary principal, Tom Moore has a strong literacy push in his school that is built upon his own teaching career when he was influenced by Dan Fader's *Hooked on Books* and filled his classroom with books. He continues this today as a principal in a unique manner. An avid reader, he purchases several hard-covered novels each month which he then donates to the school library to support young people as readers. As well, he has bought a movable bulletin board for each department and a subscription to a national newspaper. He encourages teachers to clip articles, editorials and pictures from the newspaper that highlight their particular discipline and to mount them on the bulletin boards each day. This way, students can note the contemporary effect of literacy in their lives.

Concluding Thoughts

It is helpful and fruitful to look at product — *what* an effective school looks like, but it may be more useful to focus on process — *how* a school can become an improving school. To greater and lesser degrees, principal leadership, teacher knowledge and skills, a professional community, program coherence and technical resources already exist in all schools. It is now a matter of strengthening and sustaining these factors as girders for literacy-based school success that is based on solid research exploring different approaches to literacy development.

In the light of data from Carol Rolheiser and her teams' studies of literacy-based school change in three school districts, it is clear that principals who are working to develop knowledge and skills in their staffs are seeing changes in their teachers' attitudes towards teaching literacy. In turn, they are seeing changes in their students' attitudes and abilities in reading and writing—even in those with the challenges of a new country and a new language. The remaining challenge for most of these schools seems to be eliciting greater parental involvement in and parental support for literacy initiatives.

Ultimately, it is the personal satisfaction of becoming readers and writers that enables students to continue their efforts to become literate. Once a school leader ensures that the proper supports are in place for this to happen, success can be achieved in creating literacy-based school change.

Suggestions for Professional Reflection

- What are your own beliefs about helping children become readers and writers? How does your philosophy of literacy learning affect the programs in your school?

- What is your role as a professional development leader? How do you determine, organize and implement professional development in your school community?

- How can the staff at your school take ownership of their professional development so that everyone wants to participate and it is significant for the school's overall literacy goals?

- What mechanisms does your school have in place for sharing and discussing books and articles of interest? How could these methods be made more effective?

- How can discussion on useful sources of information be more sufficiently focused? For example: Do teachers try out some of the good ideas found in these resources? Are there good sources of information that staff are overlooking?

- How can your school present its curriculum for literacy growth so that parents will understand the program and support the teachers? For example: Are there articles and books that could be made available to parents?

- What can your school do to include parents in a significant way in literacy initiatives?

- How can the school honor each family's way of life, while still developing a sense of school community? What changes might be necessary to promote multicultural awareness and respect for literacy development in all children?

- How can you include volunteers in the classroom to assist staff and students with various literacy activities? In what ways might parents, student teachers, high school students, older student buddies and invited guests contribute?

- What will be the benefits of volunteering for the volunteers, the teachers, the students and your own work as an administrator?

Suggestions for Professional Reading

- Fullan, Michael. *The New Meaning of Educational Change.* Third Edition. New York: Teachers College Press, 2001.

As a classic guide to school reform, Fullan's book adds to his pioneering work on school change. In the book, he provides a full and detailed picture of the shifts in school reform in the new millennium in an up-to-date reference for the educational innovator, as well as offers significant insights into the complexity of reform and recommends practical strategies for lasting improvement.

- Harwayne, Shelley. *Going Public: Priorities & Practice at the Manhattan New School.* Portsmouth, NH: Heinemann, 1999.

This resource provides a toolkit for building literacy change in schools. In her book, Harwayne offers detailed planning, organizing and implementing strategies to create literacy success in schools. Harwayne, through her own modeling of a true literacy principal, teaches us how to orchestrate a culture of change in schools.

• Lyons, Carol and Gay Su Pinnell. *Systems for Change in Literacy Education: A Guide to Professional Development.* Portsmouth, NH: Heinemann, 2001.

The authors offer specific suggestions for planning and implementing a literacy professional development course in this book. They present everything you will need to implement literacy change in a school from the necessary materials, to where to find them, to what the best activities for effective, hands-on practice are and how to develop in-service courses. The book enables staff developers and teacher educators to help teachers become effective in their teaching of reading and writing processes.

• Robb, Laura. *Redefining Staff Development: A Collaborative Model for Teachers and Administrators.* Portsmouth: Heinemann, 2000.

In this book, Robb advocates meaningful change that takes into account the culture of the school community. She promotes a process of professional development in which teachers reflect, listen and respond. Robb encourages teachers and administrators to grow into professionals by demonstrating how to start, maintain and assess success through such ongoing strategies as study groups, coaching, and peer mentoring and evaluation. The book features transcripts from interviews, teacher conversations and student conferences, as well as an appendix of reproducible forms for self-evaluation, study-group documentation and one-on-one conferences.

• Schwartz, Susan and Mindy Pollishuke. *Creating the Dynamic Classroom: A Handbook for Teachers.* Toronto: Irwin, 2002.

This is a valuable resource for both new and experienced teachers. By highlighting their own understandings, Schwartz and Pollishuke help teachers make links between philosophy and practice. The authors offer practical strategies on timetabling, instructional strategies, organization and classroom atmosphere, as well as outline a multitude of ways to put their ideas into practice.

Carol Rolheiser and Karen Edge

Dr. Carol Rolheiser is an associate dean at OISE/UT, as well as an authority on literacy-based school change, teacher change and cooperative learning. She is the lead writer on three reports dealing with literacy-based school change at the district level. Karen Edge is a researcher and a co-writer of the reports. Here they speak about their findings in regard to some of the factors necessary for literacy-based school change.

Leadership

• In our different research projects, we examine shared leadership, which does shift some of our thinking from the traditional roles of principal or vice-principal leadership within a school. In many of the initiatives that we are observing, where there is a literacy coordinator, we are examining how a shared leadership role for literacy works within the school.

Obviously, there are certain responsibilities that a principal has, such as greater accountability for certain aspects. However, literacy leaders can have other responsibilities. In this way, the staff views leadership around literacy as being a shared leadership role. The stronger the relationship between the roles of principal and literacy leader, the more impact it can have on the success of a literacy program. This is a true shift in our traditional ways of thinking about educational leadership.

• Shared leadership is not about assigning power to a role; rather, people assume a leadership role through their actions and because of their background experience. How these people engage with teachers, the status that the role assumes, the symbolism of that role and the respect for that role — these are really grounded in what they will bring to that role as individuals.

For example, we found many factors that were connected with the success of literacy coordinators on literacy teams. It included such things as how able they were to bring a sense of not having their own agenda to the teachers, but one based on their support of the identified needs of the teachers. Since they are interacting with teachers, they come to know what needs are being expressed, and they begin to muster their support, conceptually, as opposed to saying "We are doing big books, and I am going to come in and help you implement big books." Effective literacy coordinators have a stronger template of what might be valuable in supporting and urging people along the literacy continuum. Not only are they making connections to teachers' needs, but they also have a strong "teacher" sense of what might be helpful. They can feed that information in, using their own professional knowledge and practice to guide the learning process.

- In our literacy-based change report, we shared with staff from all the project schools what we viewed as super-accelerators—the things that really made a difference in literacy change in schools. The number one was the literacy coordinator. We wanted to communicate the message, both at the district level, and with policy makers, that this role has significant impact on literacy change in schools: an on-site person engaged in job-embedded professional learning for teachers; a resident authority.

Teachers' Knowledge, Skills and Dispositions

- You need to develop the school's capacity to have an impact on student achievement by keeping a clear focus on the quality of the teaching, of the literacy curriculum, of instruction and of assessment. But in order to develop a school's capacity, you need to develop the teachers' knowledge, skills and dispositions. The professional community calls this "The Collaborative Work Environment." This process allows teachers to work alongside one another, creating a culture of collaboration. As they look toward program coherence with a focus on literacy, that literacy focus acts as an integrator, helping teachers handle what is often felt as fragmented teaching duties and professional overload. In fact, as you are working toward program coherence, within the area of literacy, other aspects in the school are being affected positively.

Professional Development

- Another super-accelerator for change involved opportunities for teacher cooperation within the school culture, for planning and working together, with literacy coordinators creatively advocating rescheduling to ensure that there was planning time. One school made that a priority — finding joint time for teachers to get together and plan and have professional learning opportunities. They generated both the schedules and strategies that they needed for success. We are going to send these results out to all of the schools in our districts to share the wisdom that grows from participation: this is what teachers value and want.

Program Coherence

- Educational change is not about starting with a restructuring mandate where every school will have a literacy launch on such and such a date so that everybody can collaborate during that time. Rather, the staff members need to determine what they value, such as joint planning time, and from that, the desire grows to determine how that can come to fruition.

- We found that to build a creative curriculum requires a clear vision. You need to have your staff rallied around clear goals, and let your staff provide collaborative and collective leadership, with the teachers involved in making decisions on how they are going to focus their school change.

- We worry that district and provincial or state procedures either bring coherence and/or work against it. For example, there can be a literacy coordinator in a school working well with the principal and having great effect. But if the district decides to eliminate the literacy coordinators for the next year, that will have a huge impact on school progress. That is why it is important to have across-school sharing, to create advocacy and to create awareness. That is why we are involved in educational research — to feed this information to the policy-makers.

- The underlying principle for success appears to be related to program coherence. In whatever way schools choose to do it, they are then saying: How do we make literacy learning happen from one grade to another? How do we ensure that teachers have a common language? Where do we put the budget for books — a library specifically for leveled reading? Teachers need to feel that they are investing in literacy. Making budget decisions for thousands of dollars represents visible support, and actually builds a cooperative work environment. All of this builds momentum as you engage a variety of stakeholders in literacy-based school change.

Technical Resources

- Another significant factor is technical resources. Teachers need support in the case of literacy, such as having sets of leveled books. All of the successful schools we have observed have in common a strong curriculum and instruction focus, centred around good literacy initiatives and strong assessment programs. As leaders, you are building school capacity to enhance instructional quality to support student achievement.

CHAPTER TWO

Understanding Literacy Principles and Practices

I spend time as a team member with the teachers talking about particular individual students, their progress and their development, as well as what questions teachers have, what is happening in the classroom program, what isn't happening, and what we can try to do to reach that group of students. What are the best techniques for making the program rich and full? How do we identify what we are doing well, and what we need to improve? Deciding what to teach is essentially guided by the model of reading development adopted by the school.

Kathryn Broad, elementary school principal

Changes taking place within the field of literacy education do not entirely result from theoretical or methodological shifts, but also from shifts in the pedagogical infrastructure of elementary schooling. As we discussed in Chapter One, the shifting administrative paradigm directly affects how your staff teaches literacy and your students learn to be literate. However, it is also necessary to consider: What will be the base upon which you can place your new role and responsibilities?

In deciding what needs to be taught and how it should be taught to encourage literacy growth, it is important to consider questions such as:

- What is currently known about literacy teaching and learning?
- How do we define "reading"?
- How do people learn to read?
- What is decoding?
- What is phonics?
- What is reader response?
- How do teachers accommodate for special-needs students in early reading?
- How do people learn to write?
- What components are necessary for an effective literacy program?

- How can principals work with colleagues and parents to create an optimum literacy environment for students?

Certain lasting beliefs and understandings underpin effective literacy teaching and learning. These include:

- Every child can learn to read and write, given time and support
- High expectations are fundamental for all staff and students
- Schools and classes are organized to reflect a commitment to maximizing student learning time
- Learning to read and write are processes brought to life by effective literacy teaching
- Each staff member makes a difference
- Professional learning is an ongoing and essential aspect of continuous improvement
- A whole-school and community approach involving students, teachers, parents and the community consolidates student learning
- Working in collaboration with families not only strengthens the nexus between school and home, but also offers additional opportunities to promote high expectations
- Student performance is significantly influenced by teachers' standards and expectations
- Every learner is different and we should use whatever means and methods we have at hand to facilitate student learning and achievement

As discussed in Chapter One, literacy success hinges on the creation of a culture that is receptive and responsive to a whole-school commitment. In short, literacy initiatives of any kind are only as effective as the people participating in them. Therefore, as leaders committed to literacy-based school change, it is essential to tackle such sweeping questions as:

- What is valid literacy teaching?
- What are the components necessary for literacy teaching?
- Does your staff have a common language and a common set of goals?
- Is your teaching staff interweaving informal assessments with more formal assessments?
- What model of literacy governs your overall program?

In this chapter, we set out to consolidate an understanding of the principles and practices upon which successful literacy initiatives can be based if everyone is committed to the process of literacy-based school change.

Cueing Systems for Reading

Reading is an interactive process in which the reader uses a variety of strategies for ensuring that comprehension occurs. In order to make meaning in print, all readers blend four cueing systems: pragmatic, semantic, syntactic and phonographemic (phonics). Pragmatic and semantic cues help readers to use syntax and language patterns to predict words and phrases; phonics cues help readers to test predictions for unrecognized or confusing words in order to construct or confirm meaning.

It is important to help young readers become aware of how using the various cueing systems can help them find meaning in text and support their reading growth. Young children already have some of these strategies, and may use them to figure out individual words or phrases. The process is more complicated, however, when they must apply strategies to words embedded in a text, especially unfamiliar words within a text that is outside their frame of experience.

A reader uses the four cueing systems simultaneously to varying degrees. Proficient readers use a minimum of cues, while less experienced readers or readers who are reading a text for a specific purpose may use more cues to help them determine meaning. Limited readers often tend to use phonics cues as their primary strategy. When these readers are reading difficult texts, they, in essence, may need to decode the majority of words they meet. This limits the amount of comprehension that occurs as a result of the reading — the more a child must decode individual words in a text, the less meaning she or he may take away from the experience.

A proficient reader's recognition of words is so immediate and vast that they rarely notice their use of context cues. Their rate of recognition is directly tied to the amount of reading they do — the more a reader reads, the greater the automatic sight vocabulary. A parallel situation exists for those who read a variety of types of text — as they increase their exposure to text types, their recognition of patterns and structures specific to a genre of text increases. Knowledge of patterns is reinforced when writing is combined with reading — children then have the opportunity to put into practice their awareness of how print works. However, even proficient readers may sometimes miss interesting turns of phrases or special nuances because they are processing text at a speed that does not allow for subtleties. Revisiting or working with the text may increase both comprehension and the metacognitive awareness of experience of the text.

It has been proven that strong literacy programs at the primary levels that incorporate all four cueing systems can dramatically reduce the number of reading problems experienced by today's adolescents and young adults. To do this, educators need to focus on the following core elements of literacy teaching:

- Alphabet knowledge
- Knowledge of sound-letter correspondences
- Automatic sight words
- Reading for meaning
- Numerous opportunities for reading many types of books
- Increased teaching time and extra resources devoted to at-risk readers
- A secure environment that encourages children to grow as readers and writers

Critical and Creative Comprehension

When readers read, are they always able to make sense of what they are seeing in print? Do they connect to what the author is saying or do they think about what she or he is saying? Are the author's words or ideas too far removed from their own experiences? The question remains for teachers: How can they assist children in making sense of what they read, so that their personal understanding and satisfaction will grow and deepen from the experience? This is what is meant by "teaching comprehension."

Reading comprehension or textual understanding occurs when readers are able to interpret written symbols in order to make meaning. A reader internalizes the accrued meanings and relates these to previous knowledge, experiences and texts read before. Comprehension is a cognitive, emotional process, and thus, it is difficult to assess. Yet its presence or absence can be determined to some extent when teachers:

- Watch and listen to children reading a text
- Ask children to describe what they have read
- Discuss books that children are reading with them
- Encourage children to share their responses to what they have read

As will be discussed in more depth in Chapter Four, these informal ways to assess children's comprehension can be combined with more formal assessments to provide teachers with a picture of children's levels of comprehension with particular texts. Teachers can then assist children with strategies that enhance comprehension, helping them make meaning before they read, as they read and after they read.

Everyone's experience differs. It is important for teachers to keep this reality in mind as they work with groups of children so that they don't present only one interpretation of a story. Instead, teachers must share their expertise in such ways that support children and encourage their learning.

In order for readers to understand a text, they must be able to relate it to other texts they have read and to life experiences, thereby combining the knowledge gained from this text to their knowledge base. The strength of these connections relates directly to children's level of comprehension. If students cannot connect the reading to personal aspects of their lives, their level of comprehension will suffer just as it will if they cannot connect the text to others they have read.

Response to Text

Response activities allow children to develop insights into other worlds, to notice and accumulate new words and language patterns, to learn to discuss ideas from texts with confidence, to analyze and form generalizations from texts, to apply new learning to their lives and to become members of a literacy community. For example, a good story provides a powerful context for looking at how words work. Limited readers, in particular, need to see the richness of literature response, and to recognize that a story is only a beginning point for expanding ideas and increasing language strengths. What children do after reading should relate to what they have read, and could include such activities as a simple retelling through writing to writing in their dialogue journals.

If teachers were able to observe the thought processes of proficient readers, they would notice that such readers think about a book before they open its cover, then they draw on their knowledge base to identify the type of text and the strategies they will need to read it. As proficient readers begin to read, they watch for visual cues (e.g., pictures, subheadings, etc.), look for main ideas, confirm initial predictions, relate text to what they know, look for details that link to existing knowledge, anticipate what will come next, monitor for comprehension, use information from all cueing systems judiciously, as well as use contextual cues and occasionally word analysis to understand new words and concepts. After reading, these readers need time to reflect on the text, to relate ideas to their lives and to consider the implications of the author.

It is essential for teachers to support response behaviors in young readers, for these strategies ensure that children finish reading a text richer for the experience and with an expanded knowledge base on which they can draw. To do this, it is crucial to know children's:

- Interests and strengths
- Methods for making meaning
- Preferred reading materials
- Overall approach to the task of reading
- Strategies used to help them read
- Receptiveness to our attempts at helping
- Ability to relate new information to old

With this information in mind, teachers can extend children's learning by helping them to develop response strategies that will enable them to negotiate meaning making in a more efficient, deeper manner.

Schools need to help children develop into independent, purposeful readers who will think carefully about what they have read. Often, readers in trouble make little sense of what they have been decoding, or they choose to ignore meaning making completely, and give up in frustration as they fail at word calling. All children need effective comprehension strategies as they grow into independent readers and writers. To enhance these, teachers need to promote thoughtful interaction with what is being read through response activities. This, in turn, allows readers to be able to select relevant, significant information from the text, make sense of it, and integrate it with what they already know into a personal construct of knowledge.

Stages of Reading

Most children follow what can be considered a continuum of reading acquisition; however, they do not always master skills in order. That is, they may have difficulty with one strategy, yet will have gained another typically evidenced by a more fluent reader. Competencies vary according to the text being read and the situations in which children find themselves reading.

When teachers assess children's reading ability, they need to consider where the majority of the behaviors fall on a particular place in the continuum. Then, they need to watch that children make gains that will move them into the next stage of reading.

Children progress at their own rate and in their own style. In the past, readers who progressed at a slower rate were often labeled (e.g., learning disabled, dyslexic, attention deficit disorder). However, it is now known that if teachers can identify the various stages of growth, then they can have a much clearer picture of the problems and what each child needs to do to build strength as a reader.

Since reading is an individual process, one of the best indicators a teacher can use to assess a child's growth is his or her own development throughout the year. In order to do this, it is necessary to establish a baseline of skills and knowledge. In this way, as teachers assess children through the year, they can return to the baseline to see where each child has made gains.

The sections that follow provide a brief overview of the five stages of reading to help establish the baseline of skills and knowledge referred to above.

The Early Reader

Early readers, who are sometimes referred to as prereaders, enter kindergarten with some of the skills and concepts they need to become readers. These children generally enjoy reading, since most of their experiences with texts have involved being read to by family members or caregivers. Books, then, represent pleasure and entertainment for them. Many children will have favorite stories they like to hear again and again. These readers have a sense of story and enter into stories readily.

Early readers will often pick up a book and approximate reading by holding it the right way, stopping the reading while they turn the page and finishing the story exactly on the last page. Such imitation is not without value. Through this, children learn that texts give readers cues to reading, that print on a page matches certain words, that pictures support the story, that books are read from front to back, that text flows from left to right and that reading is an authentic activity. When children "read" books in this way, they are preparing themselves to become readers.

Early readers know that print carries meaning and they are aware of sources of print around them — in books, on products, on labels, on signs, etc. While they recognize many of these words in context, they may not carry over this knowledge when they see the words in isolation. These readers may not know how sounds are represented by letters. Phonemic awareness — how sounds combine to make words — and phonics — how words are written on a page — will develop during this period.

Phonemic and phonics instruction, if it is to be effective, should occur through real reading activities, such as using rhymes, songs, patterns and word games. These activities focus children's attention on sounds and the corresponding letter or letters that represent them. It is only when children have a knowledge of sound-letter correspondence that they can begin to read and write independently and transfer knowledge from one situation to another.

The Emergent Reader

Emergent readers, like early readers, enjoy listening to stories and have favorite books that they seemingly never tire of. Children at this stage know that books can provide them with entertainment and information and they see themselves as capable of reading them.

These youngsters have refined their knowledge of how books work, and realize that the purpose of print is to record or share meaning, and that it is fixed. They are beginning to rely on semantic and syntactic cueing systems to predict events, and can retell sequences of events. These children are interested in developing their print abilities. They like to have their stories transcribed, which they can read back to a teacher or parent.

To help emergent readers develop knowledge of how writing reflects spoken words, it is necessary to create environments where children are surrounded by print. Teachers or parents need to show examples of how print is used and give children plenty of opportunities to read books successfully, particularly pattern books and books with detailed illustrations. Shared reading, of course, brings these books alive and directs children to focus on functions of print. Finally, publishing children's own stories gives them real reasons to write and reinforces the major purposes of writing — to record and to share.

The Developing Reader

Developing readers can read some texts independently and successfully. Children at this stage of reading often enjoy books by a favorite author, including books in a series, and it is during this period that children come to recognize characteristics of various genres. Using this knowledge, and their experience in reading, they begin to develop a personal literary taste.

At this stage, their knowledge of sound-letter correspondence is growing, and they can recognize and write letter groups such as blends and digraphs. Their knowledge of sight words is also growing, and they can read these words in both familiar and unfamiliar contexts.

As they read, developing readers use all four cueing systems to help them make meaning. They are able to self-monitor their reading, identifying and correcting miscues, and can substitute words that make sense when they are unsure of a text. At this level, children are reading silently. Some children may still finger-point or say the words softly to themselves. As their reading ability develops further, they will discontinue these practices.

To help developing readers in their literacy development, they need to consolidate a strong sense of story. Teachers can build upon developing readers' enjoyment of independent reading, particularly with familiar texts, as well as their interest in discussing stories in small groups, and the value they place on connections between reading and writing. As part of their literacy program, teachers should introduce chapter books and simple novels and ask students to retell the plots of stories they have read. To imbue a meta-awareness of texts, children at this stage need to be encouraged to recognize characteristics of genres of texts. As well, they need to increase knowledge of literary elements and the materiality of texts (e.g., the cover, illustrations, etc.). Developing readers should also recognize phonics generalizations and have a growing vocabulary.

The Fluent Reader

Fluent readers have arrived at a point where they have built up an extensive sight vocabulary and thus are free from the time-consuming word analysis that may have occurred at previous stages. These readers can read a range of texts for a variety of purposes, read silently, link new information with existing knowledge and adjust their style of reading to reflect the type of book being read.

This is a critical stage in reading. Some children may begin to lose their enthusiasm for reading because books may appear too challenging or they no longer find themselves as captivated by story. In these cases, we must select books that children enjoy and that they can read successfully, all the while avoiding habits and classroom routines that may give reading activities the "appearance" of a choice (e.g., routine comprehension questions). Children need to continue to confirm reading as an act that entertains them, that brings them satisfaction, that adds to their knowledge and that is undertaken for genuine reasons.

Just as they are becoming independent in their reading, so, too, are they becoming independent in their writing. These children are learning to write in a variety of forms for a variety of audiences and purposes. In addition, they are improving the quality of their written work through editing and proofreading and are mastering the conventions of the language.

The school's role is to help children develop those strategies that will increase their reading and writing fluency. Teachers can do this in part by identifying genres that appear appealing, by demonstrating behaviors they consider useful (e.g., proofreading written material), by conferring with children on an as-needed basis, and by acting as a resource to help them rediscover the joys of reading.

The Independent Reader

Independent readers read texts independently and silently. The style of reading they choose reflects the material being read and these readers monitor their reading for understanding.

These children can read a range of books, as well as novels that reflect other cultures, other times and other ways of looking at the world. They are capable of interpreting complex plots and characterization and need to be challenged to move ahead on their own, using fiction, nonfiction and computers.

To further the development of independent readers, it is important to encourage them to read a range of texts in a variety of ways, through such means as independent reading, shared reading and literature circles. Since their writing often reflects their reading knowledge, they can be encouraged to respond to texts read in innovative ways.

The "English as a Second Language" Reader

These readers face a special challenge. Although they share their peers' reading tastes, their level of English precludes them from reading many age-appropriate texts. These children generally do not want to read books that are read by younger children. High-interest, low-vocabulary novels were developed to fill this gap, but did not prove to be a great success, with their general lack of plot and character sophistication. What then do teachers give these children that will appeal to their humor, their sense of adventure and their thirst for a good story? How do schools teach them to read?

First, teachers need to realize that it is important to honor each child's culture. By providing an atmosphere where these students see their past experiences as valuable to their learning of English, they have in place a set of skills and a knowledge bank on which they can draw as they learn the language. Indeed, they may benefit from being able to speak and write in their home language as they become accustomed to their new surroundings.

Second, it is essential to welcome these children into the school and make them feel a part of the school culture. Where possible, teachers may wish to pair a child with no English yet with a child who shares the same home language who has acquired some English. This buddy can introduce the new child to the physical layout of the school, its schedule, its resources and its extracurricular activities, as well as provide a model for language-acquisition success.

Finally, it is imperative that ESL readers get experience with more than just simple texts. By giving these children the same books as others are reading, then structuring the learning so that they can receive assistance and support as they read, these students can sustain interest while advancing their language skills.

Snapshot of a Literacy Principal

Each year, principal Ann Christy had beautiful and intricate designs painted on her arms by parents in her school's ethnic community. She also invited guests from the community, such as singers, storytellers and authors, to come to the school. These were important components of the celebrations in her multicultural, urban school.

The Reader in Difficulty

The factors that explain why some children are "at-risk readers" are as varied as the children themselves. Some may have medical difficulties, challenges at home or attention deficit difficulties that impede their learning, while others may learn at a slower rate than their peers, including both those experiencing problems in particular areas or in all areas of learning. Some children may progress at a "normal" pace for awhile but become blocked at a particular point in their learning. Whatever the reason, teachers need to observe and assess these children to decide on the support they most need.

Teachers can often help these children by spending time with them individually or, for brief times, in small groups where they share the same level of literacy development as other children. It is of particular importance to read aloud to these children, read with them and listen to them read. Teachers can also assist at-risk readers by giving them quiet reading time, by helping them to identify the purposes for reading, and by making obvious the link to activities that make experiences with print meaningful and real.

Snapshot of a Literacy Principal

At a school we recently visited, we observed that twice a week at noon hour, the principal plays basketball with those grade seven and eight boys who are working in a group for troubled readers. The activity is a strong motivating force for the students.

Reading Intervention

Research shows that there are certain factors that impact on literacy. These include:

- Poor readers read less than their peers
- Poor readers are constrained by a lack of vocabulary development and world knowledge
- Poor readers often experience reading in negative, passive and inefficient ways

Based on studies of large-scale initiatives over the past decade, such as Slavin's *Success for All, Reading Recovery*™ and Crevola and Hill's *Early Years Literacy Project*, the earlier you intervene with at-risk readers, the greater the improvement. Early intervention has repeatedly been shown to have a substantial impact on children's reading progress.

According to Jane Hurry of the Institute of Education in Great Britain, research evidence demonstrates that successful reading interventions require:

- One-to-one tutoring in a broad curriculum
- The inclusion of different genres of texts in a variety of groupings
- The incorporation of writing—particularly related to spelling and word-level work
- Explicit phonics teaching connected to the content of the text

In her article, Hurry maintains that although we need to acknowledge the contributions of meaning-based reading by always having a language context, there has to be a phonological element to any intervention.

In identifying a framework for intervention, it is important to focus on the following aspects:

- An intensive literacy program
- Effective teaching
- Assessment

An Intensive Literacy Program

An intensive literacy program includes a combination of phonics teaching alongside meaningful and purposeful literacy activities. There are certain key principles that are fundamental to this approach:

- Understanding that print carries a message
- Learning the relationship between letters and sounds
- Developing sight vocabulary
- Learning letter formations and spellings for writing
- Monitoring comprehension and inference skills

Some of the more successful interventions have been ones that merge a phonological approach with a meaning-based approach. What is also increasingly important is a writing component, including spelling awareness.

Effective Teaching

Research and practice have shown us that one-to-one teaching instruction in reading and writing is the best vehicle for success in literacy. As discussed above, intervention programs should also be intensive and instituted as early as possible.

The following are the critical issues in terms of teaching strategies for reading interventions:

- Increase the amount of time devoted to teaching literacy
- Use a one-to-one approach as it has been proven more reliable than group programs

- Make professional development a component of the intervention process to ensure that the implementation of programs like *Reading Recovery™* are an integral part of the overall school program

Assessment

Through assessment we not only establish what pupils know, but also what programs will befit their needs (e.g., phonemic awareness, word recognition, comprehension skills, etc.). Most importantly, assessment charts student progress. Susan Schwartz, whose comments are featured in Chapter Four, maintains that knowledge about assessment and evaluation is key to planning and monitoring all literacy initiatives.

Assessment should be used to inform the teaching decisions about particular interventions. Chapter Four provides a comprehensive look at the role of assessment and evaluation in all aspects of literacy teaching.

Models of Intervention

Below, we have identified some interventions that have proven successful with at-risk readers, based on the principles set out in the previous section.

Phonemic Awareness

In *Phonemic Awareness in Young Children,* Marilyn Jaeger Adams presents an intervention program intended for use with kindergarten, first-grade and special-education students.

Each chapter of the book is designed to lay the groundwork for the next chapter and includes the following: listening games, rhyming, words and sentences, awareness of syllables, initial and final sounds, phonemes, introduction of letters and spellings, and assessment of phonological awareness. Within chapters, items are sequenced in order of complexity or sophistication (i.e., there is a developmental continuum embedded in the book's structure). Assessment activities help teachers evaluate language and listening skills, and the assessment forms can be photocopied for frequent use with large groups of children.

Reading Recovery™, a framework for reading development conceived by Dr. Marie Clay, proposes that there is a key acquisition period in the first two years of formal schooling. During this time, children develop a set of strategies for making meaning from texts. Once children pass through this stage, they have a repository of reading strategies that they can use as they become independent readers. As Clay observes: *During the acquisition phase the novice reader is not only learning words or letter-sound relationships, but is also learning how to use each of the sources of information in texts, how to link these to stored knowledge, and which strategic activities make "reading" successful.*

In the *Reading Recovery*™ program, children requiring intervention meet individually with a specially trained teacher for thirty minutes daily for an average of 12-20 weeks. *Reading Recovery*™ identifies those children having difficulty early, before problems become consolidated. This early intervention is supplementary to classroom instruction. The major direct purpose in identifying students for this program is to prevent reading difficulties at an early stage before they begin to affect a child's overall educational progress.

Writing Development

Quality writing occurs in classrooms where students write about things that matter to them, and where a language-rich, supportive environment fosters their desire to see themselves as writers and increases their ability to capture their ideas and feelings proficiently. It is important for children to have real purposes for writing and to speak in their own voices with clarity and accuracy. Writing may not always be easy or fun, but it can be satisfying and purposeful.

Teachers have not always counted all of the writing events that occur in classrooms as acts of written composition, but they are. We have at least replaced the inappropriate subject term *creative writing* with *writing*, which opens the door for exploring the many different functions of writing, including reporting, creating, persuading, note-taking and describing, to name just a few.

To encourage writing growth, teachers should encourage students to write frequently during the day in a variety of situations: for example, note-taking during a mini-lesson; working on an idea web for a social studies project; completing a final draft of an independent piece. Students need to realize that only the last type of writing mentioned here requires extensive revising and editing — that we "publish" our writing when we have something special to share and to keep. Chapter Three describes some strategies for helping your teachers implement the writing process.

Snapshot of a Literacy Principal

Over a series of Saturdays during the year, principal Roy Howard drove groups of grade six students to the museum in a large nearby city, followed by lunch in an interesting restaurant. The students' experiences resulted in all kinds of writing, talk and further research, which they then shared with Roy.

Spelling Development

Proficient spellers have a high degree of competency in frequently used words, and find multiple resources for the spelling challenges that occur in writing. In order to become better spellers, students need to raise their spelling consciousness. The more exposure students have to reading and writing, to the strategies of spelling and to a variety of spelling resources, the more they will reinforce and strengthen their spelling patterns. Research has shown that spelling is developmental and increases and improves over time.

Teachers need to keep the requirements of standard spelling in perspective and assist students in learning to spell with a variety of strategies. Each new piece of information gained about how words work alters the students' existing perceptions of the whole system of spelling in English. Sometimes, students may appear to regress as they misspell words they previously knew, but they may be integrating new information about words into their language background.

Spelling is a complex cognitive process learned over time and bound in with all the other language experiences that change us — the books we read, the stories we tell, the friends we know. Spelling is part of the whole of language, and while teachers may ask children to focus for the moment on one aspect, they must always remind themselves to connect that part to the whole of language, so that patterns and information sink into children's long-term memories. In her book *Spelling in a Balanced Literacy Program*, Clare Kosnik explains: *Linking spelling with reading has a two-fold benefit. The words students meet in reading provide words for study. It is not just the content of the stories that makes reading and reading instruc-*

tion useful, it is also the development of reading skills and strategies that can be used in other subject areas. As students have more experiences with print, they build a bank of knowledge about words.

By organizing spelling mini-lessons and demonstrations that focus on spelling problems students are experiencing (e.g., doubling final consonants, adding *-ing*), teachers can address spelling patterns for the whole class or small groups. This models an approach to solving a problem that can be verbalized and visualized, and students can learn how effective spellers use words. Brief conferences with individual students can help them come to grips with troublesome words or patterns. More strategies for spelling growth are offered in Chapter Three.

Models of Effective Reading and Writing Programs

The list of programs that follows emerged from our research inquiry into literacy programs that have proven effective with students. In researching exemplary reading and writing programs, we examined three main areas:

- The philosophical framework of each program and its implications for teaching and learning
- The methodology of use required for implementation
- Assessment and evaluation components

What unites the programs we deem "effective" is a whole-school approach to changing literacy achievement in a district, state, province or country, based on many of the components of literacy-based school change described in Chapter One. Our selection of programs encompasses international literacy initiatives that have proven successful in Australia, Canada, Great Britain and the United States.

We also highlight reading and writing programs that do not provide prescriptive methodologies, but instead offer guidelines for teaching practice. This approach requires professional development and support services for teachers to implement them effectively — reading and writing programs are only as effective as the principals and teachers working with them.

Each program we selected is based on an approach to the teaching of reading and writing that advocates students having ample opportunities for engaging in meaningful reading and writing activities. The programs also incorporate opportunities for students to learn through talking with others. In all of these programs, literacy skills are carefully articulated and are connected to the actual processes of reading and writing.

Administrators may wish to consult this section when considering an early reading program which fits their own and their staff's approach and/or philosophy of practice. We have divided our list of exemplary programs into three distinct models of literacy as interpretations of literacy teaching and learning:

- Balanced literacy model
- School change model
- Literacy framework model

Balanced Literacy Model

A balanced literacy approach promotes reading skills and literacy among school-age children based on the characteristics of reading stages: early, emergent, developing, fluent and independent. A balanced literacy framework entails a whole-class approach to reading development that requires strong organizational skills to assess students' learning needs, to plan instruction based on these needs, and to set up learning stations and strategies that support a literate classroom. The premise underlying programs that follow this model is that students need an environment that is organized, stimulating and psychologically comfortable to learn effectively.

The 10 components of a balanced literacy program are:

- *Read aloud/Modeled reading* — teacher reads selection to students
- *Shared reading* — teacher and students read text together
- *Guided reading* — teacher introduces material at students' instructional level
- *Interactive reading* — teacher and students read and discuss story together
- *Independent reading* — students read independently
- *Write aloud/Modeled writing* — teacher models and teaches writing strategies
- *Shared writing* — teacher and students collaborate to write and teacher acts as scribe
- *Guided writing* — teacher reinforces writing skills and students do the writing
- *Interactive writing* — teacher and students choose topic and compose together
- *Independent writing* — students choose topic and write at their independent level

A balanced literacy format emphasizes speaking, listening, presenting, writing, reading and viewing. The classroom set-up can include a whole-group area, a small-group area and learning centres such as a reading area, a writing centre, a cross-curricular centre, computer stations, a creative arts centre, a communication area/post office and a listening station.

The Toronto District School Board's *The Early Years Literacy Project* is based on a balanced literacy framework and promotes the creation of administrator, literacy coordinator and teacher capacity to build, implement and monitor a literacy initiative in a school. It is premised on a model of school change devised by Dr. Peter Hill and focuses on three primary areas of school change and improvement: leadership skills; mentoring and coaching skills; and literacy program planning, assessment and implementation.

There are 93 public schools in the Metropolitan Toronto Area currently involved in the *Early Years Literacy Project*. The program emphasizes professional development, alongside the expertise of literacy coordinators trained in *Reading Recovery*™ and the administering of the Observation Survey as the core of the initiative (as opposed to a set of materials to deliver the program).

The *Early Years Literacy Project* initiative hinges on the principal and literacy coordinator relationship, wherein the principal is accountable for effective implementation of the initiative, while the literacy coordinator receives the necessary professional development and subsequently coaches, mentors and partners with kindergarten and primary teachers during the literacy time. Teachers implement the components of balanced literacy and provide focused instruction during a two-hour literacy block. All teachers involved in the project are expected to refine and expand their repertoire of effective assessment and instructional understandings and strategies.

What is pivotal to the *Early Years Literacy Project* is intervention, monitoring and assessment. Hence, all teachers from kindergarten to grade three assess the students in their classes twice a year using a variety of assessment and evaluation strategies, but in particular, teachers may opt to use the *Developmental Reading Assessment.*

School Change Model

There are literacy initiatives and early reading and writing programs that have proven effective which emerge from models of school change developed by theorists working in the area of policy and school change. As is outlined in this book, a literacy-based school change model advocates a strong balanced literacy program that operates within a new infrastructure of administration.

Michael Fullan's involvement with the *National Literacy Strategy* in the United Kingdom serves as an example of improving literacy rates by making changes to the administrative infrastructure of schooling. In an article profiling the success of Britain's program, the *National Literacy Hour*, Fullan attributes the success to six critical elements:

> *There are six critical elements to their (i.e., National Literacy Strategy) approach: First, set ambitious standards; second, devolve responsibility to the school level; third, provide good student achievement data to schools and provide clear targets; fourth, invest in the professional development of teachers; fifth, establish transparent accountability systems so everyone from administrators to the general public can see how well schools are doing; and finally, intervene in school boards in inverse proportion to success (successful schools and districts take on leadership roles; failing schools and districts receive targeted attention to turn them around).*

The *National Literacy Hour* is based on the objectives of offering focus and direction in literacy teaching and learning. Its rationale is to provide a practical structure of time in which to teach literacy. It is set up in this way:

- Begins with fifteen minutes of shared text work which represents a balance of reading and writing
- Is followed by fifteen minutes of whole-class word and sentence work

- Is followed by twenty minutes of group and independent work with mixed ability groups (some doing guided reading and others completing a writing activity)
- Ends with a whole-class discussion in which the teacher reviews, reflects upon and consolidates all teaching points

Literacy Framework Model

There are several reading and writing programs, spearheaded by theorists in the field of literacy, that have proven effective with students in a variety of contexts. Research demonstrates that such frameworks have proven more effective in children's reading comprehension than other reading programs on the market. We have identified two programs that fit this profile: *Success for All* and *The Four Blocks*.

Success for All is a schoolwide reading program that incorporates tutoring and family support services along with classroom teaching. The major components of *Success for All* are:

- Story-related activities
- Direct instruction in reading comprehension
- Independent reading
- Listening comprehension
- Writing

In this program, students work together to improve strategic reading and comprehension skills. The writing program concentrates on creative writing and responding to literature.

With an emphasis on oral language development, *Success for All* also includes: story telling and retelling (STaR), emergent reading, rhyme with reason, shared book experience and Peabody Language Development kit. The second level of the program emphasizes a balance between phonics and meaning using both children's literature and stories which have phonetically regular text, along with 50 minutes of shared reading daily. The third level emphasizes cooperative learning.

The Four Blocks program provides several varied opportunities for all children to learn to read and write. It is arranged into four blocks: working with words; self-selected reading; guided reading; and, writing. *The Four Blocks* aims to make each block as multileveled as possible. It provides additional support for children who are struggling, as well as additional challenges for children who are independent readers. At-risk students can be supported by intervention programs while participating fully in the program.

There is no ability grouping in *The Four Blocks* program. The blocks can be scheduled in any pattern to meet the needs of individual classrooms. The structure of the program is as follows:

- *Working with words* — In this block, the children work with the Word Wall, then they work on the phonetic patterns of high frequency words for reading and spelling activities.
- *Self-selected reading* — A teacher starts this block by reading aloud. The students then read a self-selected book on their own while the teacher conferences with individual children.
- *Guided reading* — This block aims to give children opportunities with different genres to teach reading comprehension. Whole class, partner and small group formats are used with membership in various formats, changing often to maintain the multilevel methodology. This is the most difficult block to maintain with a mixed-ability group.
- *Writing* — Each day this block starts with a mini-lesson. The teacher then helps students revise, edit and publish. The writing block is carried out in "writer workshop" fashion.

Concluding Thoughts

Although many of the principles and practices foregrounded in this chapter derive from the strength of research and information on the content of literacy education, they have been framed within our overall goal of promoting literacy-based school change.

As a literacy principal, you should understand and be proficient in issues tied to literacy education. There should be a shared vision in your school of what people need to know to organize and manage a comprehensive reading and writing program that includes literacy events across the curriculum and opportunities for development as individuals, as part of small groups and as part of a literate community.

Schools need teams of teachers to design and implement programs that support each child's development over the years. As lead voice in your school, you create the foundation for building the capacity for a literate community.

Suggestions for Professional Reflection

- What would you and your staff consider to be the "best possible" literacy curriculum you could ever imagine? What resources would you need to support your program?

- What would the students achieve in this "best possible" literacy curriculum? How would the staff facilitate their development?

- How do individual teachers currently establish their timetables in your school?

- How integrated is the school day?

- What literacy materials are presently used? Do they form the basis for the curriculum or are they seen as isolated resources?

- Are reading, writing and talking the centre of the curriculum?

- How can the learning achieved by staff members who have taken in-depth professional courses in such areas as writing, children's literature or drama education be most profitably shared with others?

- How can the staff at your school take ownership of in-school or district-wide workshops to make sure the events are significant to their needs?

- How can you facilitate the attendance of your staff at educational conferences that are coming up to support a new literacy vision?

- What areas of change could you and your staff control in trying to institute a new or modified literacy curriculum?

Suggestions for Professional Reading

- Booth, David. *Guiding the Reading Process: Techniques and Strategies for Successful Instruction in K-8 Classrooms.* Markham, ON: Pembroke, 1998.

  This is a no-nonsense exploration of the latest and most successful approaches to teaching reading. In the book, Booth sorts through the mass of information available and gives teachers practical strategies and techniques that will support elementary students on their journey toward becoming independent readers.

- Bouchard, David with Wendy Sutton. *The Gift of Reading.* Victoria: Orca Book Publishers, 2001.

David Bouchard, a former principal, writing with Wendy Sutton, argues with persuasive power that all people who live or work with children must become readers themselves and must take an active role in turning children into readers.

- Cummins, Jim. *Negotiating Identities: Education for Empowerment in a Diverse Society.* Second Edition. Toronto: Ontario Institute for Studies in Education, 1996.

This book focuses on how power relations operating in the broader society influence the interactions that occur between teachers and students in the classroom. The author notes that teachers have considerable control over how they structure their interactions with culturally diverse students. He describes how educators and students together can create a classroom where everyone feels a sense of belonging.

- Cunningham, Patricia; Moore, Sharon; Cunningham, James and David Moore. *Reading and Writing in Elementary Classrooms: Strategies and Observations.* Third Edition. New York: Longman Publishers, 1995.

This resource puts forward the latest research and practical strategies for developing literacy in elementary classrooms. The book presents activities and strategies to organize, predict, monitor and generalize from print. The author team offers imaginary literacy settings as indicative of how literacy should be taught and learned.

- Harwayne, Shelley. *Lifetime Guarantees: Toward Ambitious Literacy Teaching.* Portsmouth, NH: Heinemann, 2000.

Lifetime Guarantees is a guidebook on how to help children become literate. Harwayne, a former principal, presents teaching strategies to use with a variety of literacy students (i.e., those above and below literacy targets). As an expert in the field of literacy teaching and learning, Harwayne offers a whole-school program that teachers can adopt as a framework that is grounded on the reality of classroom work.

• Jobe, Ron and Mary Dayton-Sakari. *Info-Kids: How to Use Nonfiction to Turn Reluctant Readers into Enthusiastic Learners.* Markham, ON: Pembroke, 2002.

Info-Kids explores children's interest in nonfiction/information books. Based on classroom experience, the authors present case studies of students who opt for nonfiction books over other types of texts.

• Routman, Regie. *Conversations: Strategies for Teaching, Learning and Evaluating.* Portsmouth, NH: Heinemann, 2000.

Conversations offers field-tested teaching ideas, detailed strategies, reviews of theory, teacher-crafted lessons and lists of annotated resources. Education authority Regie Routman believes that dialogue incites learning. The book was written in part to spur teachers to clarify their own learning, challenge assumptions and take initiative in their professional development. Routman shares her own experiences and resources through narratives, anecdotes and examples from students' work so that we can question, modify, validate and change our own practice.

Kathryn Broad

Kathryn Broad was a principal at a rural JK-6 elementary public school in an amalgamated school board with 50 elementary schools and 12 secondary schools. Here she speaks about the experience of her school's journey to set up an effective literacy program.

Creating a Vision for Literacy

• I was a principal for five years and during the last two years there was an emphasis on two specific areas: reading and writing development. We came to think of literacy as communication in all of our curriculum areas, so that communicating and learning became important aspects of our work. We looked at our grade three standardized test results and we realized that students were not as proficient in communicating their learning as we thought that they could be.

• From the beginning, we focused on what we call "Learning and growing together." That was our mission statement. The teachers in the school were used to being involved with parents. We had an extremely strong volunteer program and we trained volunteers to help in classrooms with reading and writing. We could identify the priorities in our school — improving learning in literacy, community involvement and students becoming responsible for their own learning. Everybody in our school community knew what the goals were.

Implementing a Literacy Initiative

• In deciding how to help the students who were not becoming literate, I attempted to spend time on the team with the teachers, talking about particular individual students, their progress and their development, as well as what questions teachers had, what was happening in the class-room program, what wasn't happening, what we could try to do to reach the students, what the best techniques were for making the program rich and full, and how to identify what we were doing well and what we needed to improve. At a special education meeting, we would discuss students with severe difficulties in literacy. We had a *Reading Recovery*™ program in the school, but we were considering what we could do with those other children, the ones that were not benefiting from either our classroom programs or our special programs.

- At parent council meetings, we would look at grade two results and we would identify what things we wanted to do. We noticed that some students didn't read at home and determined, "Let's have a homework club" or "Let's have a reading club after school." We identified those volunteers who would come back and work with our children after school in an "after-hours club" and the parents did much of the monitoring. Students spent 45 minutes to an hour, with homework and reading activities at that time.

- There was an opportunity for a parent to be trained in a program called Learning and Reading Partners. After she returned, she offered, over the next couple of years, meetings for parents, training them with aspects of the program, helping them to see what literacy learning meant, so that they could help their children. It was a wonderful resource to have in the school.

- We did not have an effective program of reading assessment in our board. What we had were individual teachers who would do useful conferring with students, but we wanted to know where individual students were in terms of end-of-the-year assessments. As we changed our direction, we asked the students to identify areas of growth that they felt they had achieved, and even the youngest ones could talk about what they had learned in various areas. We didn't have every single child go through a particular critical mass reading test; we were not at that stage. But we wanted to identify areas of strengths and weaknesses that we could work on with students at risk in literacy.

Examining the Role of Leadership

- Many principals didn't choose a leadership role thinking that they would also be the curriculum leader in the school. But rather than having to be a literacy authority, they came to understand how to support and manage and provide for the staff who would be the expert teachers.

- For me, leadership is learning about your circumstances, your community, your students, your staff and all of the people you are working with. If you have a framework that opens up communication, those things that are required by headquarters will fit. However, during the time that I was a principal, and in conversation with teachers, the job has become more complex, and the time to accomplish tasks is shrinking. There is a broadening of what is expected, as in the new documents that come from the Ministry. The principal is the person responsible for health and safety, for staff members *and* for literacy development. While I think all of those things have merit, I'm more likely to spend my time on the issues of learning, with all of the staff, the students and the parents.

• I would want principals to have a basic understanding of literacy: What do you know about literacy, as a principal, as a teacher, as an educator? Where can you find the theoretical framework for the understanding that you need in order to feel confident as a leader on a team? What do you know about school change and literacy initiatives? Do you know, in your school, who the struggling readers are? Do you know who the successful readers and writers are? Do you know why? Do you know who the teachers are on your staff who are successful teachers of literacy? Do you know how to create networks that let that expertise be shared?

Managing Change

• In our school, we used the same kinds of processes for literacy change as with any kind of change. You first identify what you are going to work on, and then you determine the steps you are going to take. We needed to build resources, particularly with reading and mathematics curricula. We decided, as a school, what we needed. For example, we agreed that we wanted every child to have a personal dictionary. Then, we looked at what things we really wanted to maintain as a division or at a specific grade level.

• As a leader, you really have to know what is important and what is valuable; you have to really spend time deciding on these issues. You do have to talk to your colleagues constantly — how are they managing? You do have to find colleagues that are similarly minded and you have to really learn to communicate with your staff and your community what you have learned. As a new principal, that learning curve is straight up, so there are bound to be mistakes, but you hope that you have a supervisory officer who will help you to see the broad picture and the bigger horizon. You do have to read new articles and books, and listen to guest speakers.

• Most of all, you need to communicate with parents: "This is what we are working on/Look at what's happened here/Look at what this means/These are the steps we want to take/How can you help us?" The community becomes part of the solution.

CHAPTER THREE

Implementing Successful Literacy Initiatives

We started the literacy project my first year in this school. It was a perfect opportunity as a new principal to affect the culture of the school. Often, you don't want to institute too many changes, because teachers may feel that you are not taking account of the wonderful events that have already been going on in the school, but with the literacy project, there was actually an outside push from the board. The principal then has to look for support for helping teachers handle the accountability that new pressures bring, and find balance.

Steven Reid, elementary school principal

Now that we have taken a macro view of the factors necessary for, or at least conducive to, creating literacy-based school change, as well as some of the principles and practices that underlie literacy teaching and learning, we would like to offer some practical strategies for implementing successful literacy initiatives in your school.

A literacy-based school stresses the unity of learning through language. It looks at how children learn and how teaching practices affect their learning. Literacy is a necessary part of all curriculum areas, which in themselves can provide the context for much of the literacy and language use and growth that occurs. Indeed, literacy learning takes place naturally and continuously across the curriculum as children approximate, explore and evaluate. Whether in informative or entertaining contexts, children must see literacy as a source of personal satisfaction.

Language is acquired through use, as those who have learned a second language well understand. Literacy-based teaching strategies grow out of building a curriculum on the way children actually acquire language proficiency — by talking, reading and writing through need and desire. Whatever the label we give literacy teaching, it can become a metaphor for change — a call to question, examine and reassess assumptions, and to reflect on what we are doing as educators. Teachers and principals need to engage in dialogue with learners and be open to learning about children, about reading, about writing and about learning itself. They must also engage in dialogue with one another, observing, coaching and learning through the creation of a community of professionals, just as in classrooms they strive to create communities of learners.

Teacher education programs are beginning to require personal awareness of and reflection on what makes a good teacher. Teachers must feel they can effect change in the classroom. They must also realize that their own learning does not end when they leave university. They must be ready to explore new approaches to learning, classroom planning, effective practice, and continuous assessment of how children are learning rather than looking at test results. Supportive administrators and colleagues, who share their convictions and work with similar approaches in their own and other schools, can help build on successes and failures.

Snapshot of a Literacy Principal

At his school, principal Lorne Browne used to bring his guitar and perform folk songs for a different class each week, incorporating his hobby with school work. As a result of distributing song sheets to the students, many read the words as they listened.

Supporting Reading Success

For most people, reading is a vital part of life, both in their personal lives and in their work lives. Teachers need to establish environments and reading experiences in their classrooms and in the school that can help children develop competence, as well as positive attitudes toward reading.

Young children, in particular, must have plenty of opportunities to read and meet with success early in their school years in order to appreciate the value of becoming independent readers. To learn to read, all children need to experience effective models of writing — from computer instructions to history books to adventure novels — and to witness the numerous purposes of reading.

There are several crucial elements necessary for putting in place a sound reading program. These include:

• Ample time for reading, writing and discussion opportunities throughout the day

- An abundance of quality children's literature — fiction and nonfiction alike
- Guided reading experiences where print is examined with care and precision
- Reading in a variety of groupings and ways (e.g., independent, partner, small group, whole group, reading aloud)
- Ongoing assessment to determine and advance children's reading development

The sections that follow and a large part of Chapter Four provide strategies for making sure the above elements are addressed.

Selecting Books for the Classroom

The majority of teachers strive to select the best books for their classrooms. They look for materials that face up to contemporary social issues and that draw children to authors and books beyond the popular bestsellers. Most classrooms are full of resources for readers beginning to feel success, mature readers, interest groups, individuals with particular concerns, gifted students needing enrichment and children beginning to work in English.

Many children meet books in their homes from babyhood and, for them, sharing a variety of books with loving adults is a normal experience. Others meet books for the first time in school and, if they are to become lifelong readers, it is of particular importance that these students read more than school texts. The presence of a wide-ranging array of books in classrooms helps children to see what they read in school as "real" and reading as a lifelong activity.

A nucleus of books chosen with the varying backgrounds and stages of development of the children in a particular class is central to a classroom reading program as it offers each child a good start for satisfactory reading experiences. Having familiarity with this portion of the classroom library, the teacher can then recommend books and discuss them with the children. Likewise, children can begin to recommend titles they enjoy to each other, discuss their personal reading with others and return to favorite titles and authors.

There are tens of thousands of books for children today. The challenge is to choose wisely. This task raises questions such as:

- What should the selection criteria be?
- Should teachers have read each selection?

- Should teachers choose children's favorites, critics' favorites or their own?
- How can teachers represent positive role models, children with special needs and the multicultural diversity of our communities?
- How can teachers balance classics from the past with modern selections?

The answer to most of these questions is that children need to experience *all* types of books: classic and brand new; predictable and challenging; hard-covered and soft-covered; poetry and prose; fiction and nonfiction; by award-winning authors and classmates; related to the curriculum and irrelevant to it; popular and little-known; single works and series; picture books and novels; short stories and anthologies; for boys and for girls; folk tales from their own and other cultures; magazines and newspapers; as well as talking books, films of books and books about books. Ultimately, it is up to each teacher to use his or her professional judgment, based on personal experience and/or consultation with reputable sources, to choose the books most suitable for his or her class's needs and interests.

Snapshot of a Literacy Principal

A principal colleague always kept an old briefcase in his office full of picture books, and would offer this resource to new substitute teachers who were sent to the school — a welcome beginning to a strange setting.

Addressing the Needs of Different Readers

As has been discussed already, children do not progress at the same rate through the stages of reading. It is the school's job to take all children from where they are and help them progress toward independence. The following are some strategies you may wish to share with teachers in order to address the needs of various types of readers.

STRATEGIES FOR OVERALL READING GROWTH

There are certain strategies that teachers can use to help students become better readers, regardless of where they might be in their reading development. These include:

- Basing teaching on a sound theory of how children learn, in particular, how they learn to read
- Selecting texts that children can read successfully on their own and that will make them want to read other texts
- Providing opportunities for children to read increasingly difficult texts
- Encouraging students to reread texts on occasion for the sake of developing fluency, and to read selected texts and parts in order to develop varied responses (e.g., to examine theme, author style, etc.)
- Ensuring that children always read to make meaning and that they find significance in what they read
- Modeling the use of strategies for growing as a reader, and modeling the use of self-assessment strategies to monitor this growth
- Assisting children in using such techniques as visual information, sound-letter correspondence, analogies and words within words to advance knowledge about language
- Helping children to connect the processes of reading and writing through cooperative writing activities and through the creation of significant written responses to what they have read

STRATEGIES FOR READERS IN DIFFICULTY

Readers in difficulty often require more assistance to achieve growth than children who are progressing as expected through the stages of reading. This can range from additional help in the classroom and at home to the kinds of intervention outlined in Chapter Two. Here is an overview of the necessary supports for this type of reader:

- Programs that stress strategies for growth
- Extensive assistance as they extend their abilities
- Additional one-on-one conferring and demonstrations where needed
- Texts that are predictable and that contain easily discernible patterns (especially for young readers in difficulty)
- Activities to build letter and word patterns
- Opportunities to incorporate new sight words into speech and writing
- Time to respond to reading selections
- Occasions to reread texts, both for pleasure and for the development of fluency

Factors Affecting Reading Comprehension

The Child
- An interest in and appreciation of the text
- Connections made to the text from both life and literacy experiences
- Familiarity with the ideas that are represented in the text
- Awareness of the characteristics of the genre (e.g., report, novel, poem)
- Feelings of success and competence as a reader
- An understanding of the goal of reading a particular text selection
- Responsibility for choosing the text to be read
- Opportunities for responding to the text through discussion, writing, etc.
- The attributes, opinions and behaviors of peers during reading activities
- The conditions surrounding the event: a private reading experience, a collaborative experience, a public shared experience, a performance, or a test
- The time limits for accomplishing the reading

The Teacher
- Pretext support for setting the stage for reading
- Careful selection of the material for interest and ability
- Provision of a sense of ownership of the reading experience to the child
- Opportunities for building motivation for engaging the reader in the activity
- Design of an organization that supports intensive and extensive reading
- Regular monitoring of young readers in order to help them
- Prompts offered as strategies used to support the young reader while reading the text
- Support of independent reading (e.g., a tape of the book)
- The teacher's relationship with the young reader (e.g., tester, mentor, facilitator)
- Creation of follow-up activities that promote reflection, rereading or revisiting of the text

The Text
- Qualities of the language of the text that encourage a particular reader
- Genre of the text (e.g., narrative, lists) that was selected
- The complexity of ideas presented in the text for the particular reader
- The demand on the reader's background experience
- The inference load on the reader
- The level of vocabulary (e.g., unfamiliar words, context)
- The illustrations that support the experience of the text
- The skill of the writer in involving the reader and in presenting ideas in meaningful and well-crafted text

- Encouragement to develop literacy habits such as browsing, reviewing and selecting to support the development of a personal taste in literature
- Varied opportunities to experience success in reading and bolster their confidence as readers
- Real reasons to read and write

Snapshot of a Literacy Principal

Ivan Thompson worked as a tutor with an at-risk child every day that he could for fifteen minutes. By the end of the year, he was known by every troubled reader as someone who would help them. In addition, he became very knowledgeable about new and supportive reading strategies.

STRATEGIES FOR ESL STUDENTS

The major obstacle in achieving reading growth for English as a Second Language students is an unfamiliarity with the vocabulary, structure and patterns of the English language, as well as inexperience with the culture in which the language is used. The following are some strategies that your teachers might find helpful in addressing the needs of ESL readers:

- Pair ESL readers with buddy readers, preferably other ESL readers who have developed reading ability in English and can foster the reading skills of their partners
- Include plenty of demonstrations for the entire group so that ESL readers do not feel that they have been singled out
- Include a range of reading materials in the classroom that reflect and honor other cultures
- Provide a range of reading experiences, including shared reading, guided reading and group read-alouds so ESL readers can experiment without a fear of failure
- Find ways to draw on children's knowledge in their first language in learning English
- Tape stories and novels children are reading and make these tapes available to all children so they can use them as needed
- Encourage ESL readers to complete written responses with a partner or as a member of a small group
- Make ESL learners aware of response forms that do not rely only on writing, such as drama and visual arts

- Make parents a part of their children's reading program by discussing strategies and goals of the program, and what they can do to help their children read at home
- Encourage ESL children to get involved in community projects and events that can provide significant opportunities for learning language

Incorporating Assessment

In order to design effective reading programs, teachers need to know the progress of individual children, their reading strengths and challenges, the strategies they use, their use of cueing systems, the types of books they want and need, their attitudes toward reading, as well as the strengths and weaknesses of particular teaching methods and programs. Ongoing assessment and evaluation is a necessary component of a strong reading program — so vital, in fact, that we have devoted all of Chapter Four to the topic.

To help you monitor the overall effectiveness of reading programs in your school, we have provided the observation schedule shown on the opposite page.

Building a Classroom Reading Community

It is not enough to address just the strategies necessary for individual growth as readers. Principals also need to encourage teachers to establish a reading community with the whole class. By doing so, children have the opportunity to:

- Participate in the ongoing literacy life of the classroom
- Come to value reading in a more global way
- Begin to support one another in developing the attitudes and strategies required as lifelong readers/writers
- Benefit from teachers as models of literacy as they share the kinds of literacy activities in which they believe

One way of building a reading community in the classroom is to use a variety of groupings for reading activities. The process of learning to read is similar to the process of learning to talk — both involve immersion in a language form. In the case of reading, children need to listen to stories read aloud, read with family members and members of the community, read on their own and see others reading in order to become better readers.

Reading Observation Schedule

- Are teachers modeling reading through significant and frequent read-aloud sessions, incorporating different types of texts and styles in community-building literacy events?

- Are children reading often throughout the day in all curriculum areas — not just in language arts?

- Do children have opportunities to read in shared reading situations, instructional groups and independently?

- Are students engaging in significant read-aloud events, where students bring words in print to life (e.g., reading scripts in groups, participating in choral speaking and singing, sharing their research and reports)?

- Are students making their own choices about the texts they are reading much of the time?

- Are students keeping a record of their reading choices and experiences?

- Are children reading a wide variety of materials, including different styles, genres and formats, as well as being exposed to informational technology?

- Are students aware of different authors and illustrators, and are they developing personal preferences?

- Are students applying literacy strategies as they read, as well as after they have completed a text?

- Are students monitoring and repairing their comprehension as they read?

- Do students have reasons and opportunities for rereading texts?

- Are students responding to what they have read, critically and creatively, using reading journals or through the arts?

- Do students talk with others about what they are reading or about what they have read? Are they reading as "writers?"

- Are students reflecting about what they have read and using their literacy experiences in other ways?

- Do students see themselves as successful readers, growing in confidence and competence?

- Are students beginning to recognize their own growth as readers and set appropriate goals for development?

- Is reading becoming a useful and satisfying lifelong activity for students? Does reading add to the quality of their lives at home and at school?

All reading programs require a range of reading configurations, from reading independently to sharing books as a whole class. While many teachers and parents read aloud to young children, it is often assumed that older children will not enjoy or benefit from it. Children, regardless of their age, grow from hearing literature read aloud. We have only to look at the proliferation of book tapes to appreciate the pleasure of listening to a story read aloud.

Snapshot of a Literacy Principal

Barbara Howard invited different children into her office every Friday to share with her the books they were reading. She also read one aloud to them from her own excellent collection located on a shelf she had labeled "The Principal's Bookshelf."

Supporting Writing Success

Writing activities in classrooms can essentially be divided into three major categories:

- *Independent writing projects* — include regular opportunities for students to work independently on topics they usually select for themselves
- *Research inquiry* — is drawn from the curriculum, although at times teachers may assign a topic from a theme or genre the class is exploring as a community
- *Guided writing instruction* — is done with a group of writers gathered together temporarily to work on target areas of writing techniques and strategies, such as conventions, genre study or technological skills

Whatever the activity, there are a couple of significant strategies that teachers can use to help students improve their writing skills. First, connecting writing activities to the reading process where possible helps strengthen overall literacy development. When writing and reading are combined, children have the opportunity to put into practice their awareness of how print works. Second, allowing students to write about topics and issues that matter to them as much as possible provides motivation for acquiring new writing skills.

An open and accepting writing environment in a classroom is essential and should offer a range of writing experiences and products. These might include such forms as diaries, journals, letters, surveys, how-to-do books, games, resumés, bibliographies, autobiographies, lyrics, poems, articles, editorials, essays, memos, advertisements, commercials, brochures, questionnaires, petitions, dialogues, screenplays and legends, to name a few.

Implementing the Writing Process

Students need to realize that writing by definition is recursive: writers consider ideas, write drafts, revise, find more information, edit what has been written, share drafts, reorganize what has been written, edit again, consider published models that interest them, and sometimes even give up and start on another project. Much of writing is personal, meant only for a writer's eyes. This writing is seldom edited. Other writing is meant to be communicated, and students need to understand that these pieces require further consideration before publishing.

By rereading their own writing both silently and out loud, as well as conferencing with peers and the teacher, students can develop the ability to see changes they want and need to make in their writing as they refine their first drafts. It is essential to help teachers understand that revising and editing are important and essential processes for students to undertake when preparing pieces of writing for publication. Many students realize the need for editing, but have difficulty revising their ideas and changing the structure of their writing. When examining early drafts, teachers need to look beyond spelling and grammar errors in their initial conversations with young writers and help them look at the bigger picture.

In assisting your teachers to effectively implement the writing process in their classrooms, you may wish to consider some of the following strategies:

- Plan ways with the staff for them to model the writing process for their students. By sharing their own writing and reasons for writing, students can learn about the different aspects of the writing process from teachers. For example, a teacher could demonstrate strategies for revision by writing in draft form on the blackboard or on an overhead transparency.
- Decide as a staff what parts of speech or aspects of syntax teachers could focus on over the course of a year at each grade level, and brainstorm games or explorations that could help children discover how language works.

- Encourage staff to follow up on activities in various curriculum areas with collaborative group writing. For example, a group could write a summary of a science experiment, prepare a chart illustrating a concept learned in social studies or write a poem in response to a drama lesson.
- Promote the use of journals as a means for children to reflect on significant events from their lives, the books they have read and ideas for future writing. Although children may choose to keep parts of their journals private, they can be encouraged to select pieces for response from their teacher.
- Write a letter to parents encouraging them to respond to content and ideas in their children's writing and to help them with the revision process where appropriate. You may wish to hold an evening meeting to share techniques for helping children in different stages of the writing process.

Snapshot of a Literacy Principal

David Booth enjoyed reading the school newsletters from his son's elementary school. The principal approached the task so creatively, with children as columnists, parent views and community news from student reporters. The principal's own comments, which were always in his personal voice, were delightfully engaging.

To help you monitor the overall effectiveness of the writing programs in your school, we have provided the observation schedule shown on the opposite page.

Focusing on Spelling

Learning to spell is clearly related to students' general language development. Students go through developmental stages in learning to spell, but not necessarily sequentially or at the same rate. Spelling is not just memorization; it involves processes of discovery, categorization and generalization.

Spelling is a thinking process. Students learn the patterns, regularities and unique features of spelling as they read, write, play with, and attend to words. To help students grow as spellers, teachers need to draw students' attention to specific patterns or groups of words to help them see rules or generalizations. Struggling spellers need to focus on a small amount of

Writing Observation Schedule

- Are teachers sharing examples of quality writing models with the children (e.g., letters, stories, folklore, nonfiction, samples of student writing, samples of their own writing)?
- Are students engaged in writing activities several times throughout the day?
- Do students write about what matters to them and for authentic purposes?
- Are students writing in different genres and formats?
- Are students recording their personal reflections and feelings, as well as sharing ideas and experiences for future writing projects?
- Are students involved in the writing process — selecting a topic that matters to them, composing a first draft and then revising their work?
- Are students editing their final drafts carefully, using references and suggestions from peers and the teacher?
- Are students sharing their writing projects through classroom publishing and presentations?
- Do students treat research projects as writing opportunities, and follow the stages of the writing process?
- Do students draw from their experiences in reading texts as resources for writing?
- Are students becoming more aware of the craft of writing, noticing techniques authors use and trying them out in their own writing?
- Are students becoming aware of the need of writing for an audience, in other words, learning to write as "readers"?
- Do students participate in opportunities for instruction, such as personal conferences, interactive writing sessions and sessions for sharing their writing?
- Are students growing in their knowledge of how words work: keeping a personal spelling list, exploring common principles and patterns of spelling, learning more about punctuation and usage?
- Do students have opportunities to use the computer for different writing functions such as word processing, revising, editing, formatting and doing information searches?

information at a time, especially in examining connections among words and word families, and can benefit from such strategies as mnemonic tricks.

Students need to attend to the appearance of words and to check their encoding attempts. As they try to spell words, they often discover the underlying rules of the spelling system. More experienced spellers fix up their misspellings as they go along, correcting those words they already know, rather than waiting until they have finished writing. Students can benefit from learning how to do these quick checks, heightening their ability to know when a word looks right.

Before teachers tell students how to spell words, they need to ask "What do you know about this word?" and build on students' knowledge. For example, students can be encouraged to circle words in doubt. When they return to the words, they can write them over until they look correct. By considering a pattern or generalization that applies, or saying a word slowly and stretching out the sounds, students can learn to picture words "in their mind."

To assist your teachers in helping their students to become better spellers, you may wish to consider some of the following strategies:

- Provide opportunities for staff to acquire further background in spelling in order to help their students apply patterns and generalizations in spelling new words.
- Find ways to share the latest spelling research. For example, a group of teachers could read a significant article and, then, report on and discuss information with the rest of the staff.
- Suggest to teachers that as a staff they create a file of strategies and ideas drawn from or inspired by various books and articles on spelling and punctuation to help them cope with problems individual children are having with writing words down.
- Encourage staff to use spelling texts as helpful resources rather than as a complete program. Some published programs are developmental and permit student choice and can therefore help guide the learning and monitoring of student progress.
- Share relevant spelling research with your school's parents and explain how the school is assessing and monitoring children's spelling development. Suggest meaningful ways for parents to support their children's spelling growth at home.

Supporting Technology Use in Literacy Programs

As technology advances, so do our literacy practices to respond to them. Certainly, as a result of technology, there are different sorts of literacy practices employed today than there were twenty years ago. Practices like word processing, web searches, scanning documents, and even pointing and clicking and cutting and pasting are now fundamental to the writing process.

In response to this, as principals, you need to assist teachers in incorporating technology into their literacy programs. Some of the technology-related skills that teachers should include in a literacy curriculum are:

- Use the Internet as an instructional resource and for on-line learning programs
- Develop web navigation strategies with students
- Have the students use the Internet to support research and writing
- Ensure students make full use of word-processing features when publishing pieces of writing
- Encourage students to enhance their writing through fonts, color, spreadsheets, graphs and photos
- Have students share pieces of writing with other young writers on the Internet
- Allow time for students to foster relationships with readers and writers around the world through e-mail
- Encourage various forms of electronic communication through e-mail, mailing lists and newsgroups
- Incorporate CD-ROMs, videotapes and films in literacy programs so that students can access different forms of information
- Have children listen to books on tape

Supporting a Whole-School Approach to Literacy

As has been discussed throughout this book, literacy initiatives in schools are most effective if there is a whole-school commitment to creating literacy-based school change. To create a culture of change means establishing a commitment to change and a community of teachers that advocates literacy improvement. This includes not only manifesting changes in classroom space and daily routines, but adopting a new perspective on roles and responsibilities.

As a literacy principal, there are a number of ways you can promote a whole-school approach to literacy. Although most of these have been touched on already, this list provides a summary of the most important considerations.

- Review all literacy programs in the school with the staff and commit to continued improvement, planning and professional development
- Encourage teachers to constantly reflect upon and share ideas in order to plan instruction, as well as to monitor, track, assess and reflect upon student development in all areas of literacy
- Offer preparation time and professional development for staff in developing, planning and organizing literacy initiatives
- Put in place appropriate resource personnel such as staff leaders or a literacy coordinator to serve as coaches, mentors and partners for your teachers
- Make sure timetables reflect a schoolwide priority for literacy by providing hour-and-a-half to two-hour block in each class focused on reading and writing
- Explore flexible timetables that allow for each of the following in classrooms:
  - time for teachers to read to children a few times a day
  - a daily silent-reading time when children select their own books
  - opportunities for group reading and interactive response
  - book talks by teachers, students, librarians and/or visitors
  - rehearsed oral reading by the students for real purposes such as readers' theatre or reading buddies
  - reading conferences that allow teachers to observe the reading strategies individual children are using and to assess the meaning they are making as they read
  - the integration of what children read with their writing
  - time to engage in different aspects of the writing process
  - attention to how words work, such as word families, patterns and core vocabulary
- Provide assistance for at-risk students in the form of remedial support or second-language acquisition support where needed, as well as the chance to work in flexible groupings and settings with other children to reinforce particular knowledge and skills
- Ensure that all classrooms are organized for a combination of large group, small group and individual literacy activities at all times

Dear Jayshree,

Whenever I spend time in your classroom and observe your interactions with the students, I regret that I cannot spend more time with educators like you. You bring literacy alive by offering your students authentic and meaningful language events.

As a literacy teacher, you respond to student needs when they arise and you engage children in your classroom. By encouraging students like Rashid to predict meaning in stories, you provide them with a myriad strategies they can draw on when they face new literacy challenges.

Based on Monday's observation, you generate lively discussions and connect stories to the children's own experiences. Your discussion as a prelude to the story about Japanese immigrants was an apt segue into a story about emigrating to a new country. In particular, I admire the way you connected the story to your own experience so that students appreciate that you, too, know what it feels like to be inducted into a new, foreign culture.

Upon entering your classroom, I was immediately struck by the fusillade of environmental print, posters of authors, and children's work as responses to texts read in class. Having said that, given the number of English as a Second Language students you have in your class, you may want to locate some more multi-ethnic texts for your classroom library. In an effort to create an inclusive culture, I am encouraging our staff to use the halls and walls as a reflection of our community and, indeed, to promote the efficacy of cultural diversity in our school. Incorporating authors and their writings from our students' host cultures reinforces the fact that we bring our heritage to bear on our interpretation and depiction of texts.

Jayshree, your teaching is intensive and responsive. You know how to help growing readers like Kieran feel at ease with their progress. However, you may need to place more emphasis on the different cueing systems, as I noted that some readers like Marika relied only on phonics cues to guide their reading of the story. Marika sounded out four words over the course of her reading of the short passage and you did not respond in any of those instances.

Your level of engagement, enthusiasm and organization comes out in everything you do and say. By acknowledging strategies students use in their literacy pursuits (e.g., noticing first letters, searching for meaning in pictures, reading left to right with eyes, and recognizing frequently encountered words) you give students greater confidence in their reading and writing. Do let me know if there is anything I can do to help you in your teaching and learning.

With respect,
David

- Promote print-rich environments in each classroom and throughout the school in the form of: classroom libraries, references such as dictionaries and thesauruses, word lists and walls, writing rubrics, experience chart stories, information charts, samples of students' writing, banners, notices, etc.
- Support the creation of classrooms where children are immersed in a world of words through listening, speaking, reading and writing in a variety of ways
- Encourage an examination of a variety of media, such as television, radio, newspapers and the Internet, to foster literacy development
- Suggest that writing activities be connected to the reading process often so that children recognize the reciprocity of the processes of reading and writing
- Promote literacy events across the curriculum so that students see that reading and writing cross curriculum borders and that literacy is integral to all subject areas
- Foster communication and cooperation with parents throughout the school year about their children's literacy development, accepting their concerns, sharing with them significant observations and data, and valuing their support at home and at school in building lifelong learners

Creating Support Networks for Teachers

Support networks often involve the comprehensive system a school develops to help beginning teachers or experienced teachers new to a school adjust to a school's culture, administrative requirements and expectations. As Susan Schwartz explains, support networks can also create "collaborative vision" in a school. Here, Schwartz offers an example of "collaborative vision" in a school in which teachers share their expertise:

In a school I visited recently, a principal had an elaborate sharing system with teachers whereby six or seven teachers worked together for a block of time when they delivered programs to different groups of students.

In addition to in-school support, teachers also require professional support from outside the school if literacy-based school change is to be effective. The chart shown on the opposite page outlines some of the conditions necessary for providing support to teachers at several levels.

INSIDE THE SCHOOL	OUTSIDE THE SCHOOL	ACROSS A LARGER NETWORK
Set a culture for change and a desire to improve	Cultivate community involvement	Create collaborative networks for teachers by grade level and interest
Offer administrative support and leadership	Share information about successful programs	Provide sources of new information
Free up time for professional development	Ensure you have adequate supplies and materials	Provide opportunities for visitors and guest speakers
Provide effective and inviting work spaces and reading resources	Find personnel and resources to support professional development	Consult outside sources and professional materials for up-to-date guidelines on running and implementing programs
Exhibit professional materials (e.g., articles, books, etc.)	Provide training and ongoing support through outside professional development	Be receptive to research projects by districts and colleges

Using School-Based Educational Specialists

School-based resource personnel are often key to the success of literacy-based school change. These specialists may have various functions, including:

- Working in one school over time so they know the staff, administrators and students
- Continuing to teach students over time, thereby basing professional development on the particular needs of a school
- Being released from the classroom to develop and implement a professional development system that is integrated and meets a school's vision

- Having an ongoing relationship with a school and even being a part of the parent community
- Working closely with parents and having a stake in school achievement
- Gathering data, thereby contributing to research in a given area and reporting back findings to a school

The following are descriptions of specific in-school roles that principals may wish to consider incorporating as a part of an overall school literacy plan:

- *Instructional team leaders* — These people are appointed by the principal from a pool of volunteers. They set agendas for weekly meetings where teachers share ideas, discuss curriculum and ask the group to help them with specific students. Twice a month, instructional leaders share ideas with the group. They should receive a stipend for their work.

- *Peer mentors or coaches* — In this role, master teachers and less-experienced teachers with expertise in a specific area, such as language arts, are paired with first-year teachers. They can also collaborate with more-experienced colleagues who request assistance while implementing a new strategy.

- *Resource teachers* — These people are specialists in areas of the curriculum and provide positive learning experiences for mainstream teachers. These specialist teachers can work with teachers during lunch and/or during planning periods before or after school.

- *Literacy coordinator* — As a resident expert of literacy education in a school, a literacy coordinator provides in-school support for teachers as they develop and improve their instructional and assessment skills. Part of the job includes assisting teachers in implementing strategies for grouping students and solving literacy-related problems with staff. Such a resource person shares his or her knowledge and expertise with teachers and engages with parents as partners in a whole-school commitment to literacy success. As well, a literacy coordinator organizes and maintains literacy resources for teachers, including professional materials that can supplement current knowledge of literacy teaching and learning.

- *Literacy committee* — This group consists of the principal, teachers, and often parent representatives. It provides support in the form of meetings, plans long-term events and activities, and even handles some budget concerns.

• *Administrators as instructional leaders* — The primary aim of administrators as instructional leaders is supporting teachers by responding to questions and providing resources they will need to do their jobs.

Using District-Based Educational Specialists

Teachers often benefit from the assistance of outside resource personnel in their efforts to create literacy-based programs. These people may perform a number of functions, including:

- Working at the district office and spending considerable time in schools — this allows for an understanding of the school system, including such factors as politics, community, past problems, etc.
- Providing professional development for teachers at a range of schools and across grade levels
- Providing support for teacher educators working at a school-based level
- Working with administrators at a range of schools across a district so they are aware of district-wide trends, patterns and initiatives
- Specializing in a grade level, which allows for the development of a broader expertise in providing professional development in many settings

The following are specific outside roles that can benefit a school in the process of creating literacy-based school change:

• *District consultants* — Many districts hire educators to act as consultants or specialists in particular curriculum areas. These people usually work with individual teachers or groups of teachers within a school or groups of teachers from across the district to provide assistance with programming or offer professional development related to particular needs.

• *Private consultants* — Private consultants work on a "cost for service" basis and generally have a high level of expertise through constant work in many schools. These consultants often bring fresh ideas from the outside as they work independently for a professional development company or publisher. They often have access to new materials and can visit your school to organize such events as teacher-organized study groups, informal lunch meetings and consultant-facilitated study groups.

- *University-based teacher educators* — These consultants work at a university or college with whom a school may have a partnership. They can provide fresh, new ideas from outside the school and are often knowledgeable about new research and instructional strategies. They may assist in curriculum development, do field-based research in a school to contribute to the field of education, or work in partnership with a school to offer seminars and workshops. Student teachers and their advisors participate in practicum sessions in specific schools which adds support to the regular program.

Snapshot of a Literacy Principal

As part of our preservice school partnerships, we work with a principal who has created a reading tutorial program where student teachers get to work with a reading buddy for a half hour every day they are at the school. Together each child and student teacher write a summary report at the end of the five-week session that is sent home to the parents, describing and celebrating the literacy growth of their child.

Forging Partnerships with Parents

Although research has shown that it can be challenging in some districts to elicit parental involvement and interest in literacy initiatives, it is well worth the effort to include parents at a variety of levels. Once parents are presented with concrete ideas for getting involved, they often rise to the challenge and serve as important partners in the literacy process.

Parents are a child's first and most important teachers. Parents who read for their own interest, read aloud to their children, and talk with their children about reading and writing, promote literacy by conveying that reading is an important, and normal, activity. Schools should make determined efforts to encourage and broaden parents' reading with their children.

Keeping in touch with the home through interviews, conversation, reports and cooperative projects is now common practice. Many schools send home a monthly newsletter to inform parents about the upcoming month's assemblies, fund-raising efforts, excursions, birthdays and other celebrations. An accompanying calendar often highlights classroom and school events. Parents have responded enthusiastically to this type of monthly correspondence as it helps them to plan and to discuss what goes on in school with their child. Teachers who take the time to prepare these letters/calendars feel that they form a significant bridge between school and home.

In Lucy Calkins and Lydia Bellino's *Raising Lifelong Learners: A Parent's Guide*, they explore the role of parents in supporting children in their literacy pursuits. At one point in the book, Calkins and Bellino speak of supporting early attempts at literacy behavior:

> To support children's early progress toward reading, it is helpful to anticipate, watch for, and celebrate the progress they make en route to being independent readers. To do this, we must realize from the start that children often "pretend" their way toward being readers. The child who holds a book upside down and "reads" an elaborate fairy tale is on his way toward reading.

As lead voices of literacy-based school change, principals must demonstrate to parents how children learn language and develop as language users. Difficulties can arise when parents do not know about the school's philosophy of literacy teaching. Teachers need to constantly inform parents about the strategies they are using and provide careful documentation of each child's growth. Parents need to understand how literacy is the basis of the curriculum, so that when they see their children reading silently and aloud, revising, explaining and researching, they will know that their children are learning about language as they work with it.

When parents hear children read aloud chorally, see them create a poetry anthology, or receive from them handwritten invitations to classroom events, they will recognize language learning and literacy growth. When parents help in the classroom, taking part as storytellers, scribes or assistant librarians, they will see children involved in real literacy experiences. When parents see teachers' plans — with long-range goals set out — and observe careful records of children's progress, they will grant teachers the support they need to make a curriculum based on children's own language development success.

Effective school leaders recognize the strengths of a solid relationship with the community in building significant literacy programs. The following are some strategies your school might want to try to get parents more involved in a whole-school literacy commitment:

- Encourage parents to read to or with their children each day
- Compose a letter to parents inviting them to recommend books that they have enjoyed reading with their children to share with all parents

- Plan ways to involve parent volunteers in the library to shelve books, review new materials and read with children
- Institute a schoolwide program where parents can assist children who are having reading difficulty on a one-to-one basis
- Use parents as researchers by involving them in drawing up questionnaires, holding interviews and analyzing results and reactions

Concluding Thoughts

Classrooms and schools are communities of interdependent people who meet daily throughout the year for the betterment of all. As Steven Reid notes in his interview comments in this chapter, administrators and their teaching staffs need to take the time to discuss such sweeping issues as:

- What is literacy ?
- Is there consistency in our literacy programs?
- How are we using data and strategies to change programming to better meet the needs of students?

Alongside wrestling with the large issues around literacy teaching and learning, principals and teachers need to work out problems, celebrate special events, and encourage student and parent cooperation and involvement at all times. This highlights that ultimately everyone is responsible for contributing to literate classrooms and schools. Conditions for literacy are as important as the methodologies used to teach it.

This chapter set out to provide strategies for supporting growth in both the content of literacy and the creation of a culture of change. It is really only a start in becoming aware of the processes necessary for effective literacy-based school change to take place. By embracing the experiences and ideas of others, as well as conducting their own classroom inquiries, it is possible for teachers to modify and extend their methods for assisting young readers and writers. It is your job as a literacy principal to set the stage for this to happen.

Suggestions for Professional Reflection

- How does each teacher organize his or her classroom for learning in terms of traffic patterns, materials, furniture, etc? Could changes be made to make the environment more conducive to literacy learning and student ownership?

- In what ways could you increase access to learning materials for your staff that are appropriate to the development of literacy, useful at various work centres and related to classroom themes?

- How might you work with staff to ensure that multiple copies of textbooks or trade books in various curriculum areas are effective resources and correspond to the school's overall literacy goals?

- How can you help teachers to reflect on their own teaching methods, taking into account their strengths, weaknesses and biases?

- How can teachers begin to integrate the language processes of reading, writing, listening and speaking in all areas of the curriculum?

- How might you modify or change the intervention programs currently in place in the school for at-risk readers?

- How might you assist teachers in accommodating children with special needs in regular classroom programs?

- Does your school subscribe to professional resources that can add to teachers' overall understanding of literacy and aid in their practice?

- Is there a framework in place for teachers to share ideas about curriculum and classroom organization?

- In what ways can you help the wider community recognize the holistic needs of children so that you can gain support for your attempts to build a literacy-based school?

Suggestions for Professional Reading

- Booth, David. *Reading & Writing in the Middle Years*. Markham, ON: Pembroke, 2001.

  In this book, Booth presents approaches to teaching reading and writing to students in grades four to eight. Students in these middle school years are already reading and writing but they need help in continuing to develop their literacy strategies and in constructing meaning with a variety of resources. The book provides the type of support that is needed as students are faced with more reading, writing and thinking challenges in the middle years.

- Fountas, Irene and Gay Su Pinnell. *Guiding Readers and Writers Grades 3-6*. Portsmouth, NH: Heinemann, 2001.

This book explores the essential components of junior and intermediate elementary school literacy teaching. In it, the authors present the basic structure of a literacy program set within a framework that encompasses a building of community through language, word study, reading, writing and the visual arts. There are detailed sections on planning for guided reading and using leveled texts. At the end of the book, Fountas and Pinnell provide a book list containing 1000 books organized by title and level. The appendices feature such useful tools as reading and writing workshop forms, graphic organizers, and numerous lists and bibliographies.

- Jobe, Ron and Mary Dayton-Sakari. *Reluctant Readers: Connecting Students and Books for Successful Reading Experiences*. Markham, ON: Pembroke, 1999.

This book provides insights into: characteristics of each type of reluctant reader; resources and strategies to facilitate success with all students; internal and external barriers that inhibit readers; and user-friendly entry points that are sure to engage any reluctant reader. The book also includes a multitude of annotated lists of suggested literature.

- Kosnik, Clare. *Spelling in a Balanced Literacy Program*. Scarborough, ON: ITP Nelson, 1998.

This is a comprehensive guide to creating an effective and integrative spelling program as part of a literacy program. It is a resource that not only facilitates a greater understanding of the developmental stages of spelling, but also provides practical activities, reproducible assessment and evaluation checklists, a guide to spelling terminology, and a list of most commonly misspelled words.

• Stead, Tony. *Is That a Fact? Teaching Nonfiction Writing K-3*. Portland, Maine: Stenhouse, 2002.

In this book, Stead demonstrates the importance of introducing nonfiction into students' repertoire of texts. *Is That a Fact?* explores a variety of authentic purposes for writing nonfiction, such as describing, explaining, instructing, persuading, retelling and exploring relationships with others. Teachers will learn how to introduce each purpose using a variety of forms, including letters, reports, poetry, captions, directions and interviews. Other features included in the book are: practical ways for organizing nonfiction resources within the classroom; strategies for assisting children in collecting information for research; a chapter on spelling; and strategies for assessment and evaluation that guide teaching and learning engagements.

• Strickland, Dorothy; Gansk, Kathy and Joanne Monroe. *Supporting Struggling Readers and Writers: Strategies for Classroom Intervention 3-6*. Portland, Maine: Stenhouse, 2002.

Drawing on 40 years of combined classroom teaching experience, the authors explore the factors that contribute to success and failure in literacy and provide systematic and ongoing approaches for helping students who are most at risk. In this resource you will find effective teaching practices that can be implemented in a multitude of classrooms.

Steven Reid

Steven Reid is a new principal in an urban school. His school is located in a large district that has implemented an intensive district-wide literacy project. Here he discusses the challenges and rewards of being part of such an initiative.

Creating a Vision for Literacy

- Last year was our first year of the literacy project, building capacity in administrators, literacy coordinators and teachers who work with kindergarten and primary students to improve students' literacy skills. When we looked at where we were last year, some of the important questions at the time were: "What literacy programs were the teachers actually involved with in the classroom? Was there consistency? What assessment was being used within the classroom? How were we using research data to change our programming for our students? How were data being used to change the fundamental make-up of the school? How were we using media teachers, remedial teachers, etc.?

- There were also several questions that principals asked as we met at principal meetings as part of the literacy project, such as: What is literacy? What are the components of literacy? Do we have a common language as educators? Very quickly, as soon as we began our discussions, we discovered what one principal thought was guided reading was not necessarily the case for others. It became a process of investigation so that we could have a common language for literacy within our schools.

- Last year we provided professional development and dialogue opportunities for staff. We started to look at what our belief systems were, such as every child should know how to read and write by grade three. We were also buying into the fact that we, as professionals, were going to be learners together, and that this would be a journey of professional development.

- The more we talked together, teachers began to reconsider our literacy program, which to me was an indicator of success. They began to share and place new ideas within their programs. Although it started from the district project, we could see that there was also a grassroots movement— teachers were buying into the approach.

- Each of the committees that we began at the beginning of last year had at least one grade team representative. We would look at the information, we would look at goals and targets that we had been setting, and then we would go back to the grade teams, get the information, and see if there were any questions or if clarification was needed. We had representation from each of the teams of teachers, and all of us had a clear understanding of where we were going.

Implementing a Literacy Initiative

- We started the process by investigating what balances a literacy program — what it could look like. We looked at the literacy block and what needed to be in that literacy block. What should reading events look like? How does a teacher actually work with four or five students within guided reading? What else should be happening in the classroom? Instruction can't always be with a full class. You have to work with certain students who are at a particular instructional level along a continuum. We started to look at professional development for task management and activity centres. For example, how do we get students to a place where they can actually take ownership of their time — where the teacher can sit with a group of children and work with them?

- At the beginning of the district project, many of the literacy coordinators did not have a firm conceptualization of what their role entailed, and there was a lot of "trying to figure out" what they should be doing. The literacy coordinators are now developing a video so that new literacy coordinators will have clear concepts about the role, and also so that teachers will understand what they should be doing.

- Assessment was definitely an area that we wanted to investigate. Last year, we looked at various types of assessment over the year for the school, and we knew that reading was the number one priority. That was the main area of concern for our school. As principal, I knew that we did not have enough assessment data. I found that in the past, full literacy plans were made and created, and assessment was almost an afterthought. We began to focus on a school plan, a three- to five-year agenda that would actually be a working document — not just ideals posted in the staffroom.

- Everyone could see, basically, where we were. However, we wanted schoolwide data that we could pull together to identify where we were doing well and where students were at risk. ... We incorporated the data collected into a schoolwide database. We have been looking at that data now, and it's very interesting. We were able to, at grades one, two and three, identify students at the beginning of last year who were not at grade level and who were at-risk. This year, we have taken all the students who are in grades one, two and three, and we have looked at that data again. We are able to see progress early enough in the year in order to make changes.

• We have looked at some of the data that has come back from the homes and how some of our parents are working with their children. We have spent time this year with small in-service sessions for parents, only one hour in length, both during the day and after school. Parents can come in and learn more about what they can do with their children with shared reading experiences, for example. We need to build a bridge for children reading at home and at school.

Examining the Role of Leadership

• Principals are teachers: some have a strong background in literacy and some do not. Some have a strong background in assessment, some do not. These are areas, obviously, where we need a great deal of professional development. Research tells us if we as educators want to be successful with a project, the principal has to be strongly committed to bringing people together toward a common goal. It has to be a collaboration among the leaders within the school — administrators, department heads, coordinators, resource staff — to help the entire school work toward these common goals and vision.

• While there is a tremendous amount of paperwork involved within the role, that is not why principals move into it. Principals want to make a difference. They feel that they can work with staff and be curriculum leaders. Personally, I want to be working with teachers, looking at the research, examining what they are doing within the classroom, and involving them in conversations about how together we can change. I want to consider how teachers can share with each other, have professional learning teams and grade teams working together, and how I can provide professional development within the school day.

• I not only take part in providing professional development, but I continue to actively seek out professional development myself through the literacy school project — bringing back that information and making an effort to articulate, "This is what I have learned." I want to demonstrate that I am truly a learner for life. I continue to invest time reading about literacy and talking to teachers about our work. People will often notice when the principal spends time in literacy initiatives. The teachers then have a clearer understanding that I am willing to work with them. If I cannot help them, I will find someone who can.

- When we start to look at cutbacks, we see that everything slowly weighs down on the principals and secretaries to do more, spending more of the day sitting in front of the computer, reading e-mails, looking through all the documentation that is coming through various educational committees, and so on. That becomes a daunting task. You quite often feel that you are being pulled away from the classroom. I need to continually look back and revisit my priorities. As a new principal, that is difficult, because the broad focus of what is really important may not be clear and it takes some time to determine what really needs to be done today.

Managing Change

- We started the project my first year in this school. It was a perfect opportunity, as a new principal, to affect the culture of the school. The first place that we started was communicating with the literacy coordinator and developing a literacy plan for the school. We needed to be able to identify where our needs were and where we could set appropriate goals and targets. The board has targets that offer models: we considered our population of students and then set our own goals to meet those boardwide targets over time. I have so many hard-working teachers who are energizing me within the project.

- If you are setting your goals appropriately, they will be attainable first in the short term, then move toward your long-term goals. In the literacy project, we had a goal of setting up our resource room for literacy, with leveled sets of books for students to be using. That was done very early on in the year. Another goal was the professional development component: teachers were actively involved in achieving that. We can see the potential for continued growth, and we are beginning to make real fundamental changes. When I look at our school, there is no question in my mind that our teachers are taking an active interest in professional development on a daily basis, and this is certainly affecting classroom practice.

CHAPTER FOUR

Assessing from the Inside Out to Improve Literacy Standards

Principals need to understand assessment in a variety of ways. I think principals need to be really effective models of assessment portfolios and reflective practice, demonstrating to teachers that effective assessment can happen with everyone in a school, especially if the principal is modeling the process all the time.

Susan Schwartz, former elementary and secondary principal and a teacher educator

It is clear that assessment and evaluation are priorities in current literacy initiatives, and therefore fundamental to your job as a literacy principal. Assessment and evaluation take on different guises depending on the nature of the program, from informal tools such as observations or running records, to more formal tools such as diagnostic tests or compulsory standardized tests. It is essential that you, as lead advocate for your school, understand the content implications of these methods and tests and how each type supports students' learning.

Schools represent communities of independent people who meet daily throughout the year for the betterment of all. To unite your learning community, your job as a literacy principal entails building an assessment and evaluation program that represents the heterogeneous needs of its people, while at the same time establishing a common philosophy that underpins your reading and writing curriculum. The two forces can work in unison if your program of assessment and evaluation speaks to independent student needs *and* accords with the philosophy of your overall literacy framework. In their book *A Teacher's Guide to Standardized Reading Tests*, Calkins, Montgomery and Santman contend: *Schools need to reach out for tools to conduct our assessment sitting side by side with children.* What underlies all assessment and evaluation are three fundamental principles of good teaching — be active, be reflective and be collaborative.

Defining Assessment and Evaluation

There are as many views about assessment and evaluation as there are about acquiring literacy skills. Some educators adhere to a philosophy of reading assessment that only rigorous, long-standing diagnostic tests like the Gates-MacGinitie Reading Test can measure student progress. Although these tools carry some validity and reliability when combined with other methods, they should not be used exclusively as a reflection of a student's abilities. Instead, we promote adopting more of a mosaic of formal and informal assessment tools to evaluate student progress and to thoroughly support student learning.

Before outlining specific assessment tools to help your school build a strong reading and writing curriculum, we will define some key terms you will need to construct a curriculum that matches your school's, your teachers' and your students' needs. To clarify the two terms: *assessment* is the gathering, recording and analysis of data about a student's progress and achievements or a program's implementation or effectiveness; *evaluation* is the application of judgment to the data gathered and its analysis, in order to place a "value" on progress, achievement or effectiveness.

Assessment is therefore undertaken to assess the strengths and needs of a student. Essentially there are three general sources of assessment evidence in classrooms — observations of learning, products students create and conversations about literacy development. Based on such assessment data, teachers can then make informed decisions about their overall program to determine whether or not the original objectives and approaches they set out were appropriate, and to make modifications so that the program satisfies the needs of individual students and the class as a whole. Evaluation, as Anne Davies points out in *Making Classroom Assessment Work,* comes in many forms, from descriptive feedback to more formal evaluative feedback that identifies how a student performed compared to others.

The three major types of assessment that teachers should integrate into their literacy framework include:

- *Diagnostic assessment,* which can be undertaken at any time during the year to evaluate the progress of particular students and to decide whether they require some form of intervention
- *Formative assessment,* which is ongoing assessment that occurs at any time in the year to identify difficulties quickly and to provide an opportunity for immediate remedial action

- *Summative assessment,* which occurs at the end of a unit, course or program

The purpose of all of these types of assessment is to examine students' achievements in relation to some standard of excellence or in relation to some body of knowledge. The ideal program of assessment and evaluation for any reading and writing curriculum outlines a process of ongoing observations of children's development with modifications and/or interventions when the need arises. Just as we need a wide repertoire of ways to help children learn to read and write, so too we should use a repertoire of assessments to evaluate all aspects of their progress so that we take into account both their strengths and their weaknesses.

Understanding Standardized Testing

Calkins, Montgomery and Santman define a standardized test as *a test in which people are measured in a uniform way.* In their work, the authors describe "positive" types of standardized tests, such as criterion-referenced tests, and "negative" types of standardized tests, such as norm-referenced tests. According to Calkins et al., the problem with norm-referenced tests is that they are designed to produce scores that fall on a bell curve and to do this they are pre-tested by students who are supposed to represent the national average. Herein lies the problem with norm-referenced tests: they assume that all students learn at the same pace and are from a similar background. Criterion-referenced tests, on the other hand, reflect standards that have been set by such national organizations as the National Council of Teachers of English. Hence they measure what students know and can do through a variety of performances, rather than by relying solely on more of a paper-and-pencil format. What is crucial to find out about a standardized test is its construct validity; construct validity refers to how well a test measures what it purports to measure.

Provincial and state governments maintain that the goal of standardized tests lies in comparing results among schools and school boards. In theory, such an approach, as the Ontario Ministry of Education explains, *helps to identify areas that need improvement and target resources accordingly.* What "testing for a better tomorrow" means for you, as a harbinger of change, is a new dimension to your planning and monitoring of a schoolwide literacy initiative that not only matches teacher and student needs but also meets curricular outcomes and expectations. Choreo-

Testing: The Unseen Curriculum

The education ministry assured parents that tests were not intended to rank schools. But that's precisely what has happened. Now parents chase results like camp followers in search of the elusive perfect school, basing everything on a paper test. The benchmark of a good school is now marks and marks alone, rather than a big picture that includes report cards and regular communication with the teacher.

People aren't asking about the mood of the school, whether the children are happy or whether they demonstrate compassion and generosity and tolerance. Concern for the education all students receive in all schools is giving way to the hype surrounding published test results. For some schools, high scores are the result of teaching to the test, at the expense of regular curriculum.

Parents now seek out schools like the one my children attend (where I'm pleased to report kids seem happy despite increasing parental attention to marks), no longer satisfied with schools they'd been happy with until published results suggested they should feel otherwise.

And that's the crux of the issue. Test scores set up a smoke screen to hide larger issues in education, such as the crumbling state of many urban schools. Schools where children play amid a forest of portables. Schools constantly under the threat of losing music programs, swimming pools, librarians and other vital resources because strained budgets simply cannot be stretched any farther.

Then there's the way results are reached. Should two or three students be absent during testing week they are counted as not meeting the provincial standard, bringing down an entire grade's standings. Not accurate and not fair. And let's not even talk about the bills for all this testing. But the testing goes on. I saw the future recently when a friend from California visited with her daughter, who has written standardized tests every year since starting school. Annie is seven years old, with three tests under her belt. She'll write at least a test a year until she graduates. It's a frill students simply can't afford.

By Catherine Mulroney, *The Toronto Star*, Monday, May 13, 2002 graphing a literacy initiative in your school at times places you in a divided position because you face conflicts between meeting policy demands versus student and teacher demands.

Assessment is not cut and dried; it is not a process whereby you simply identify students who need help and commend those who are doing well. It is a complex and well-researched field of inquiry that defies standardization. Nonetheless, standardized testing is now part of teachers' and students' reality and hence a vital aspect of your role as a model of literacy.

Government tests are no doubt here to stay, but how we handle the process may determine many of the literacy outcomes for our students. School leaders have a significant role to play in setting the context for learning in school systems using standardized or norm-referenced assessments. To address the realities of teaching today, principals must recognize the underlying assumptions of standardized tests and decide how both informal and formal assessment methods can be built into a school's reading and writing curriculum. In the newspaper article that is reprinted on the previous page, Catherine Mulroney, a parent educational advocate, cautions us to recognize the strengths and weaknesses of the tests we inflict on our children, and to examine the resulting effects on school programs and on the culture of learning.

Assessing from the Inside Out

A fundamental part of your job as gatekeeper of literacy initiatives in your school is understanding:

- What assessments and strategies to administer
- How your teachers can teach test-taking strategies
- How to respond to asssessment measures with interventions or programs
- How increased achievement scores can lead to improved reading skills

But the question remains: What will children be tested on? And, what impact will this have on their education? We are not suggesting devoting valuable teaching time to teaching to the test, but, instead, facilitating a meta-awareness of tests, test-taking strategies, and how assessment works within a balanced literacy framework.

To create an effective assessment and evaluation program in your school you have to encourage teachers to combine a variety of informal assessments with such diagnostic tools as the Gates-MacGinitie Reading Test or the Yopp Singer Phonemic Segmentation Test, as well as compulsory tests mandated by provincial or state governments. Indeed, to tackle the challenge of more formal assessments such as annual standardized tests, it is necessary to develop a reading curriculum that works from the inside out.

When we speak of creating an assessment program from the inside out, we are referring to the assessment and evaluation that grows out of students' needs. Teachers and their principals must have high expectations for each child's success, and support development and learning with appropriate and supportive attention that embraces each child's interests and needs. The ideal school culture is one which does not highlight errors and mistakes, but instead focuses on what children can do, through observation and assessment, and recognizes the possibilities that lie ahead for each child. Teachers need to see mistakes as part of the learning process, and to use the knowledge that they have gleaned from the children's attempts in order to offer support and instruction in literacy techniques.

Anne Davies, in *Making Classroom Assessment Work,* uses the metaphor of assessment as *inukshuks* or "markers made of stone" that guide travelers to their destination. In planning a literacy initiative in your school, it may be useful to regard assessment and evaluation as navigating a course for each student. What this implies is simultaneously, and, we might add paradoxically, individualizing and standardizing. In short, ask your teachers to find the right tools to assess students' reading and writing abilities, evaluate or diagnose their individual progress, and juxtapose this against the norm (i.e., compare to results among other schools and school boards).

There is a large repository of research and writing on assessment and evaluation that comes to bear on this philosophy for assessing young readers and writers. Here, Anne Davies indicates the three salient findings about assessment that we now know due to work in the field by such researchers as Purkey and Novak; Schon; Black and Wiliam; Hurry; and Davies herself.

- When students take ownership of their own assessment, they are required to think about their learning and articulate their understandings, which correspondingly helps them learn
- When students are involved in their own assessment, mistakes become feedback and they get to make choices about their progress

- When the amount of descriptive feedback is increased and the amount of evaluative feedback is decreased, student learning increases significantly

In the end, what is clear from research, theory and practice is that it is important to assess *all* areas of children's development to improve literacy standards in your school. To do this, you need to gather information from a variety of sources, including consulting the writings of others, as well as communicating with and consulting teachers, students and parents to crystallize what exactly you need to do to create successful literacy-based change.

Deciding What to Assess

Before deciding on a particular mode or tool for assessment, it is useful to consider the breadth of what needs to be assessed in literacy. The chart shown here is derived from a report researched and written by The Center for the Improvement of Early Reading Achievement (CIERA) and is offered as an example of what needs to be assessed in the early stages of reading development. It includes five literacy categories and their constituent knowledge, skills and attitudes. Obviously, this list is merely representative of the myriad items that need to be considered at each stage of literacy development, but it at least provides a start for your school's considerations of what needs to be assessed.

Literacy Category	Knowledge, Skills and Attitudes
Concepts about print	• Has concept of letter or word • Understands directionality • Identifies parts of a book • Labels pictures • Understands letter and word order • Has a sense of story • Understands punctuation marks • Understands that print conveys meaning • Understands upper- and lower-case letters • Recognizes word boundaries
Attitude	• Has a good attitude toward literacy activities • Enjoys reading • Exhibits good reading behaviors • Exhibits good writing behaviors

Literacy Category	Knowledge, Skills and Attitudes
Reading comprehension	• Knows the topic of a book • Wants to become more fluent • Identifies own name • Is developing some accuracy • Has reading flexibility • Chooses appropriate texts • Uses book language • Monitors own reading strategies • Uses self-correction methods • Uses pictures and story line for predicting context and words • Uses print for predicting meaning of the text • Comments on literary aspects of the text • Connects personal experiences with text • Distinguishes fantasy from realistic texts • Draws conclusions • Identifies cause-effect relationships • Makes inferences • Provides supporting details • Retells • Knows the sequence of story events • Summarizes main ideas
Motivation	• Refers books to others • Is motivated to read • Uses family support and prior experience to read • Has reading preferences • Responds to literature • Reads for own purposes • Spends time reading
Metacognition	• Has familiarity with types of texts • Is able to monitor reading • Is aware of personal progress • Plans how to read • Exhibits reading-related behaviors • Self-assesses in non-language arts domains too • Self reviews • Shares with others • Executes strategies for how to read • Incorporates teacher feedback • Has writing-related behaviors

Key Modes and Tools of Assessment

- Observation
- Observation guides and checklists
- Anecdotal records
- Reading interviews
- Retelling
- Running records
- Portfolio conferences
- Reading response journals
- Reading conference miscue inventory
- Checklist of comprehension strategies
- Literature circles for self-evaluation
- Responding through visuals
- Personal response
- Reading logs
- Cloze procedures
- Profile of writing behavior
- Writing process observation guide
- Responses to open-ended questions
- Completed enterprises, such as projects, activities, assignments, reports, research, graphs, charts, illustrations
- Reading records of books read
- Writing folders
- Writing samples, such as plays, letters, stories, published pieces
- Spelling inventory
- Developmental spelling test
- Exemplars as benchmarks
- Informal and formal tests
- Diagnostic tests/surveys (norm and criterion-referenced tests)
- Standardized achievement tests

Modes and Tools of Assessment

As has been discussed already, in choosing suitable modes and tools for assessment, the goal is to create assessment-friendly classrooms where the staff understand the foundations of the reading and writing processes and incorporate techniques and strategies that enable each child to achieve success. It is with this in mind that we present a series of possible modes and tools of assessment from which you and your staff can create an assessment and evaluation program. Given the plethora of skills, backgrounds and types of learners in classrooms, it is essential to have versatility and breadth in your assessment and evaluation program. We present these modes and tools not as a prescription for assessment, but instead as a series of suggested assessment activities you can use to structure your school's reading and writing curriculum.

In the chart shown on the opposite page, we have highlighted key modes and tools of assessment that have proven successful in indicating a child's literacy progress. As well, in the pages that follow, we provide a description of some of these types of assessment for your information. We list the items both on the chart and in the sections that follow from more informal measures to formal measures of reading and writing development in order to reinforce our belief in balancing formalized approaches with daily, weekly and monthly informal approaches to assess literacy development.

Observation

When we observe children during literacy events, we bring to the process our knowledge of the theory of language learning and the practical aspects of teaching children to read and write. There are two types of observation: close observation and distance observation.

Close observation involves observing a child for a period of five minutes while she or he reads or writes. During close observation, the teacher might note such features of the reading process as: the reading strategies a child uses; aspects of the text that appear to be challenging; and, what the child does when she or he encounters difficulty. Distance observation involves watching such reading behaviors as how a child selects a book, reads independently or moves around during the activity. To observe children to a sufficient degree, teachers need to make observations of one or two children each day, or devote one day a week to observation.

When possible, teachers should tape children's discussions and presentations. Viewing the tapes away from the hustle and bustle of the classroom provides them with information relating to children's level of and type of participation in groups, the level of discussions in which children engage, and individual strengths and weaknesses.

When observing students, your staff should bear in mind the following six fundamental stages in setting a literacy program:

• Know the strategies of proficient reading and writing
• Observe and record students' interests and attitudes

- Choose appropriate procedures
- Use the procedures effectively and efficiently
- Develop appropriate strategy lessons
- Determine reporting procedures

Observation Guides and Checklists

It is essential to bear in mind that observation guides and checklists are precisely that — indicators of a child's progress. Once again, the key to any effective literacy initiative lies in combining several assessment tools simultaneously, so that no one guide can be viewed as absolute.

Checklists and guides are most valuable when they are repeated several times throughout the year. In this way, trends and progress that occur over the year can be noted. For example, in the case of reading, they can help show how a child is developing as a reader — the level of fluency, use of strategies and awareness of cueing systems. As Anne Davies notes, observations arising from checklists can be shared with children too, to encourage them to take responsibility for their learning by focusing on areas that require change.

Your teachers may wish to try a published tool such as Marie Clay's Observation Survey for assessing reading development. This informal reading assessment tool assesses concepts about print by applying a criterion-referenced approach to reading development and is targeted for emergent literacy learners. The aim of Clay's Observation Survey is to help students develop independent reading strategies such as cross-checking, self-monitoring and searching for meaning. It also measures letter identification, concepts about print, sight word reading, and hearing and recording sounds in words, oral reading and writing vocabulary.

Anecdotal Records

Anecdotal records are those that teachers make on an informal basis as they observe children in their day-to-day learning. Given the nature of these observations, many teachers choose to make notes on index cards or a small notepad. Individual cards or sheets from the notepad can then be stored in open files. A teacher may choose to observe children by groups or on an individual basis.

Students often provide a lot of useful information in inventories, and anecdotal recording is one way of keeping track of this information. Inventories, where children complete a list of their achievements, favorite activities or interests, can be extremely helpful when planning topics to explore in class. Additionally, inventories can tell a teacher about children's feelings related to aspects of their learning and information that may not be visible in class.

Ideally, children can complete an inventory like a reading attitudes inventory either in writing or orally when they begin school in September, and these can then be updated throughout the year. In this way a teacher can learn about negative or indifferent attitudes early and try to discover the reasons for these through another method such as the one described below.

Reading Interviews

What students believe about reading and reading instruction affects their decisions about strategies to use during reading. A reading interview is a series of open-ended questions designed to tell you:

- The strategies used by proficient and inefficient readers
- How students cope with difficult material
- What qualities typify "good" readers, according to students
- What reading strategies students would recommend to others
- Students' personal strengths and weaknesses

Reading interviews should be conducted in an informal setting relatively free from interruption. Notations of students' responses can be written or taped. A teacher may wish to conduct reading interviews several times during the year to determine if attitudes have changed and if there has been development in students' knowledge about the process of proficient reading.

In examining students' responses, a teacher can speculate on the ways in which their reading proficiency has been influenced by previous reading instruction. The kinds of information the interview reveals, along with teacher observations, can be used to design appropriate reading experiences for each student. As well, the results can be discussed with students to determine the different kinds of strategies they use as readers.

Retelling

Employing retelling of a text as a form of assessment and evaluation promotes a meta-awareness of text content, design and structure. It also facilitates a greater awareness of the variety of texts made available to students over the course of their learning. According to Hazel Brown and Brian Cambourne in *Read and Retell: The retelling procedure, as we define it, coerces learners to bring to their conscious awareness of many features of text structure on which they would not typically focus, or upon which they would not typically reflect.* By sharing retellings with peers, students make explicit what would previously have been primarily implicit and have the opportunity to apply their previous knowledge and experience to new types of texts.

In their research, Brown and Cambourne found that if teachers sample students' retellings over time, and use them in conjunction with other assessment tools, they can make evaluative statements about:

- Reading ability
- Knowledge of various genres
- Control of many aspects of written language
- Control of many aspects of the writing process

Retelling provides a rich and detailed picture of a student's language development over time.

Running Records

A running record, like miscue analysis, presents a record of a child's reading behavior on a specific text. It was developed by Dr. Marie Clay in New Zealand. In this procedure, a teacher sits beside a child while the child reads a text, so that both the teacher and the child are looking at the same text. The child reads a text that she or he has read before, although on occasion, a new text might be read once or twice as a final assessment of progress.

The text should be one that presents some challenges so that the teacher can observe the problem-solving strategies the child is using. However, it should not be so difficult that the child cannot continue to read. Otherwise, the child cannot put into use the strategies that she or he possesses, resorting to guessing or to sounding words out at the expense of understanding the meaning.

Based on Marie Clay's research, a teacher adopts a coding system that determines a student's reading strategies and use of cueing systems by regularly charting reading development on a running record. As a student is reading, the teacher observes closely, coding the child's reading attempts on a form using symbols Marie Clay developed as a modified reading record. In this way, a teacher acts as an observer rather than as an instructor, recording all of the information the child reads. If a child cannot continue because of a difficult word, the teacher can tell the child the word so that the reader can move forward and maintain fluency.

The most common miscues we find in running records are substitutions, omissions, insertions and reversals. They fall broadly into three categories — graphic change, meaning change and structure change. Of these three, those mistakes that result in a change of meaning are most serious, since they reflect a lack of understanding of the text on a child's part. If a child makes mistakes in all three categories, particularly those relating to meaning, and does not self-correct, a teacher can determine that the passage is too advanced for the child.

Snapshot of Literacy Principals

In one district, principals provided support for teachers by providing access to in-service on running records, learning resources for students such as "leveled" books, and specialist reading teachers. The principals themselves increased their knowledge of reading instruction by participating in a session in which they observed a teacher modeling the administration of a running record and then conducted a few running records themselves. They also met in peer groups to discuss progress in their schools, devise strategies for supporting their teachers and respond to input on school change from university staff.

Portfolio Conferences

Portfolio conferences about reading are an invaluable source of information about children's reading experiences. In this type of assessment, children bring several journal entries to a conference to discuss their growth as readers with their teachers. Informal discussion questions may relate to the number of books read, the number of books begun but not finished, and the reasons for this. Based on the results of such a conference, a teacher may conduct reading inventories and/or set new goals with students (e.g., setting a number of pages or books to be read; reading books from another genre, etc.).

Portfolio conferences can take place between a teacher and a child, between peers, or between a parent and a child. Of these configurations, teacher-child conferences are essential, peer conferences are desirable (depending on the age of the children), and child-parent conferences are recommended. The teacher's conferences with children are essential for the development of self-assessment skills. Only after a teacher conference occurs with each child should the children participate in other types of conferences. Ongoing child-teacher conferences may culminate in child-led parent-child conferences at the end of the year.

Reading Response Journals

Reading response journals contain children's ideas, reactions and opinions of what they have read. They are a way for children to organize their thoughts and to record ideas generated by a story. When children first use a journal, many simply retell what they have read. As their familiarity grows and their confidence as readers develops, children begin to use their journals as a sounding board for their perceptions and reactions. To achieve this, children need to write in their journals regularly. Their entries can take many forms, including point-form notes, webs, illustrations and notes to their teachers.

The purpose of teachers reading students' journals is to discover what children are thinking about in their reading, to help them to develop as readers, and to focus on making meaning. When teachers respond to children's journals, they can comment on their ideas and reflections, perhaps making connections between experiences and encouraging them to explore other aspects of their reading. They can also dialogue with children by sharing their own responses to a book. If the goal is to have children extend their thinking and learning, then teachers need to be genuine in their comments.

Often students and teachers write their responses as letters to each other. This format allows teachers to deepen children's thoughts, extend ideas, move into personal experiences, focus on interpretive skills, and redirect readers who have been sidetracked or confused. Journal entries can also be discussed during conferences to increase insight into children's reading.

Checklist of Comprehension Strategies

A checklist of comprehension strategies enables a teacher to observe to what degree a student is employing the strategies of a proficient or inefficient reader. Proficient reading strategies are identified and put on a continuum, which the teacher can then use as a checklist to record his or her observations of a student's reading behavior and progress. A continuum from 1 (least proficient) to 5 (greatest proficiency) works best.

On the basis of observations of a student's reading, the teacher places a check mark on the continuum at the place that most closely represents the student's use of each comprehension strategy. One checklist is required for each student. A student whose proficiency falls within the 1 to 2 range on an item on the checklist likely requires reading strategy lessons.

Literature Circles for Self-Evaluation

A literature circle typically comprises three to five children who are reading the same book and who come together in small heterogeneous groups to discuss, react and share responses. The purpose of the circle is to promote reading and responses to literature through discussions and to provide opportunities for children to work in child-directed small groups.

At the beginning, the teacher often selects the book and assigns children to groups. As time progresses, children should be encouraged to choose from among three or four books, giving them some control over their own learning, and to form their own groups. The teacher generally monitors the groups and may join a group to add to the discussion. Literature circles usually meet three times per week for a period of fifteen to thirty minutes, and can last from one day to six weeks, depending on the length of a book. Journals can be used as both a follow-up to literature circle discussions and as preparation for future discussions.

Taping a session can help the teacher to observe the dynamics of the group and the literacy behavior of its members. As well, group members can view the tape after completing discussions on the book in order to reflect on their contributions and the process. As a follow-up to that, members should be encouraged to self-reflect using their journals.

Personal Response

Personal response is an account of the transaction that occurs between the reader and the text as meaning evolves. Personal response is an essential first step in reading. Personal response reflects what a story, poem or play says to the reader and what the reader says to the story. Because of readers' diverse backgrounds and attitudes, variations in reactions to a text are inevitable and legitimate. This form of assessment accounts for and indeed legitimizes subjective interpretations of texts.

The assessment of personal response can occur as students engage in a variety of activities, such as class or group discussions or drama, art or music activities related to books. In the case of assessing personal response, it is helpful to find out where children are as readers as early in the school year as possible. This process would include an investigation of students':

- General interests
- Perceptions of literature
- Favorite books or genres
- Readiness with which they become involved in what they read
- Habitual approach to a type of book, particularly fiction
- Interpretations and perceptions of what they read

Instruments to help in this assessment might include general interest inventories, reading interest inventories, teacher/student conferences, personal reading record cards, personal response journal entries, and observations, both formal and informal. As a result of this type of assessment, teachers can direct students to further reading materials that will match their interests and ability to read and comprehend with independence. As well, teachers can help students to make stronger connections between themes and ideas in literature.

Reading Logs

By encouraging students to keep logs in which they record their reading progress in general, teachers can encourage children to reflect upon themselves as readers. Logs generally indicate the extent of growth of independence in reading as students gain confidence and skills in their ability to interact with printed materials.

To implement reading logs, teachers need to provide folders for students to keep their records. Students then bring their folder to individual reading conferences. The logs can help teachers and students to discover:

- Reading interests
- Quantity of material being read
- Breadth of reading

Depending on the results, teachers may wish to redirect students to different types of reading material in order to encourage wider reading or, if students are reading very little, may wish to administer a reading inventory to help explain why this is so.

Cloze Procedures

Cloze procedures involve oral or written deletions of parts of words, whole words or phrases in a passage of text. "Clozing," or restoring these gaps, requires children to scan the text, recognize and process contextual cues, and then choose the most appropriate word or phrase. In this way, the reader learns to use context to help figure out unfamiliar words, and it is an active and constructive language process.

Cloze activities are suitable for use at all grade levels and can help to build a number of skills exhibited by strong, fluent readers, including:

- Focus on contextual cueing systems
- Abilities to anticipate the text to make the most sense
- Interaction with text, such as searching, scanning, and thinking, that can result in making meaning with print
- A repertoire of thinking strategies
- Confidence in ability to predict in order to recognize words
- General reading ability, comprehension and vocabulary awareness

An example of a cloze activity is the following homophone cloze: I was ___ tired __ read the last ___ pages. (This, of course, would need to be filled in as: I was too tired to read the last two pages.)

Deletions can target particular types of words as in the example above, or can be made arbitrarily. Cloze procedures can also target parts of words you would like to assess and in which your students need practice. On the whole, cloze procedures are a useful way of assessing children's reading ability, comprehension and vocabulary.

Profiles of Writing Behavior

Observation of young writers at work can provide your teachers with information about students' knowledge of the skills and processes of writing. A profile of writing behavior checklist is designed to form the basis for in-depth, ongoing observation. It is a record of the kinds of behaviors and methods of working demonstrated by each student. The items on the checklist are not necessarily a list of required behaviors, nor are they behaviors to be avoided. Most writers will display all of these behaviors at some time during two or three writing sessions. Observers will need to note which behaviors are evident, and their duration, and judge whether or not they are appropriate for the particular task and stage of writing.

The observations can later form the basis for discussions with the student, and for reporting to parents or in-school review committees.

Profiles can be created at the beginning of the year to get a general picture of each child's writing behaviors and strategies. They can then be used at intervals throughout the year to monitor those students whose strategies do not seem to be productive. Profiles might be used as a basis for a sustained observation of one student, or to observe a number of students at five-minute intervals throughout a writing session to see the activities students are engaged in.

A profile of writing behavior may help answer such questions as:

- Does the student understand what should be done at each stage of the writing process?
- Does the student use avoidance strategies, such as pencil-sharpening or collecting materials, to delay getting started on the task?
- Is the student having regular conferences with peers and with the teacher?
- What does the student want to discuss during conferences?
- Does the student sustain writing for long periods?
- Is the student a confident writer or is constant reassurance necessary?
- Does the student use print sources to get information?

Exemplars as Benchmarks

In response to more structured language curriculum, provincial and state governments have produced documents which furnish examples of high and low achievement in reading and writing in grades one to eight. Exemplars are intended to serve as models for boards, schools and teachers in setting reading and writing tasks.

As the Ontario Ministry of Education explains, using exemplars over the course of a literacy initiative can help you and your staff to identify students' reading and writing levels in the following ways:

- Show characteristics of student work at each level of achievement for each grade
- Promote greater consistency in the assessment of student work from grade to grade and across provinces and states
- Provide an approach to improving student learning by showing children's written work completed at their level
- Offer clear criteria by which to assess students' written work

- Illustrate the connections between what students are expected to learn and how their work can be assessed on the basis of levels of achievement

You are by no means obligated to use a government's version of exemplars, although they do furnish a blueprint for your own development of a set of rubrics. You and your staff can cull examples of student work that match different levels of achievement and collectively create your own rubrics. For example, you and your staff may wish to collect samples of writing assignments or journal entries that show the range of writing in a given grade and bring these samples to a staff meeting to discuss and come to a consensus as to why you think certain samples belong in a respective level. Schools can thereby create their own set of exemplars that they can use as benchmarks throughout the school year.

Informal and Formal Tests

Tests, both informal and formal, are helpful when they assess learning that is measurable and when they reflect the content of the program. However, in reading and writing, many components cannot be isolated. For this reason, interpretation of tests must be handled carefully. If information gleaned from a test does not reflect a teacher's ongoing assessment data, the testing device may need to be altered. A less likely scenario involves the teacher adjusting his or her ongoing assessment.

If both the test and the instruction are sound, it is important to keep in mind that there are a number of reasons why a child may not perform well on an isolated test, ranging from a bad night's rest to a problem at home. Test results should be viewed by you, your staff and the students as a way to check the effectiveness of the program. In this way, children will feel less anxious and not be concerned that a poor test result will influence their learning for the rest of the year.

In some locations, as discussed earlier in the chapter, class-wide testing is becoming more common. Much has been made in some areas of lower than expected results, and a call for action has resulted. What educators need to keep in mind, just as in individual cases, is that a variety of factors may influence reading and writing results. One evident example is a class where the majority of the class speak English as a second language. Such a factor must be taken into account when discussing lower than expected results. It is also important to consider the fact that in such situations one test for all may not be the most effective measure.

Reading Assessment Tools

The chart that follows features current data about reading assessment tools. It is derived from various databases on the Web and from statistics acquired in the light of recent standardized tests. We hope this information will provide some help in terms of what tools teachers currently administer, what cognitive elements are evaluated, and their overall construct validity. We have deliberately chosen tools that reflect many of the principles we profiled in the other types of assessment described in this chapter.

A Sample of Early Literacy Assessments Used for Instruction	
Assessment Tool & Targeted Grades	*Parts of Literacy Assessed*
Analytical Reading Inventory (1995) — K to 6	Concepts about Print and Reading Comprehension
Clay's Observation Survey (1998) — K to 3	Concepts about Print and Reading Comprehension
Developmental Reading Assessment (1997) — K to 3	Reading Comprehension and Phonemic Awareness
First Steps™ (1993) — K to 6	Concepts about Print, Reading Comprehension and Phonemic Awareness
Gates-MacGinitie Reading Test (1989) — K to 3 +	Reading Comprehension
Motivation to Read Profile (1996) — K to 3	Reading Comprehension
Names Test (1990) — K to 3	Phonemic Awareness
Qualitative Reading Inventory (1995) — 2 to 4	Reading Comprehension
Reading Recovery™ (1993) — K to 3	Concepts about Print and Reading Comprehension
Running Records (1993) — K to 8	Concepts about Print, Reading Comprehension and Phonemic Awareness
Yopp Singer Test (1995) — K to 2	Phonemic Awareness

Concluding Thoughts

For many educators, the tasks of planning, monitoring, and then assessing and evaluating children's literacy development are complex and increasingly fragmented tasks. By complex, we are referring in particular to the challenge of assessing children's literacy skills, evaluating their progress, adapting programs to meet their needs, and ideally preserving an even progression of their literacy development.

There are four main participants who must take centre stage in assessing and evaluating literacy skills: you, the principal, as the lead advocate for a balanced assessment program; your teachers as the primary recorders of children's behavior and work; your students as self-assessors and record keepers; and your students' parents as valuable sources of information, insights and observations about their children, as well as partners in the campaign to help children become literate.

As we have tried to highlight throughout the chapter, creating a mosaic of assessment and evaluation tools offers greater precision and ultimately more support for students. A strong assessment program relies on merging a hybrid of assessment tools that speak to the multiple needs of students. To conciliate the formal with the informal, the goal should be to acquire both formal and informal data from student learning to evaluate students' attitudes toward literacy and language development and to draw conclusions about students' overall development of literacy skills.

What we hoped to model in this chapter are assessment and evaluation procedures that are student-centred, that keep language and thought intact, and that have comprehension at their centre. In addition, we have deliberately presented an overall assessment program that takes into account a continuum of assessment tools, from informal ones to formalized ones. To return to our main message, we not only need to understand the assumptions, the content, the design and the intentions of assessment tools, but also to coach children on every aspect of an assessment program.

Since we are working in a pedagogy that combines multiple and at times contrary perspectives on assessment, it is your job as a literacy principal to unify them so that all students have an opportunity to improve their literacy standards. As a starting point for reflecting on the assessment practices in your school, you may wish to consult Regie Routman's Suggestions for Fair Testing Practice shown on the following page, as well as the Suggestions for Professional Reflection offered after that.

Regie Routman's Suggestions for Fair Testing Practice

Write down your beliefs about assessment and evaluation. Do it without referring to this text or any other. Then, ask yourself:

- If this is what I believe, how am I putting these beliefs into practice?
- What can I change to make my evaluation process more effective, humane and workable?
- What are some ways I will know that my practices are effective for improving instruction and learning?

Work to ensure that your school and district testing practices are developmentally appropriate and fair to children. This is no easy matter. With so much pressure for high test scores, inappropriate practices are rampant. Get together with your colleagues.

Take a hard look at how you prepare students for high-stakes testing. While it's absolutely necessary to prepare your students for tests, is your focus and time spent reasonable? Do students understand why and what they are being prepared for?

Decide how you can adjust your daily teaching so that assessment is part of instruction and not separate from it. The traditional school structure does not build in time for assessment or stress the importance of ongoing assessment. As we did, you may want to start a study group. (Many of us met for months through our language arts support group. Without those conversations, student-led conferences would never have become a reality.)

Make sure authentic classroom-based assessments are guiding your instruction and that such assessments have priority over standardized tests. Be sure you are clearly communicating how and why you assess to the families of your students and how you use that assessment to inform instruction. Teacher assessment has been de-emphasized and devalued in the media, so we need to be outspoken on the importance and value of classroom-based assessment.

Ask yourself, "Can students apply what they have learned to new contexts?" Before students can apply what they have learned, they have to be able to problem solve, make judments, recall and transfer information and be aware of their thinking processes so that knowledge in one situation can be used to create new learning in another. Our instruction and assessment must encompass this high level of thinking if we are to equip our students to become lifelong learners.

From *Conversations* by Regie Routman

Suggestions for Professional Reflection

- How might your school begin to examine its policies and articulate a plan for assessing the progress of children in various grades and divisions?

- In what ways could your staff most effectively share the assessment strategies, checklists, guides, etc. that they have collected and find helpful for assessing various literacy concepts, skills and attitudes?

- How can teachers use ideas such as concrete demonstrations of children's growth (e.g., writing folders) for preparing for teacher-parent conferences?

- How can teachers use the questions that arise during teacher-parent conferences as a starting point for further communications, such as personal letters, newsletters, copies of articles, or student self-assessment reports?

- How can your school enlist the help of parents in the whole process of assessment?

- How might your school use occasional reading and writing assessment tools across the whole school in a way that is most beneficial to all?

- How can you and your staff ensure that in administering such tests as standardized tests that the results are seen as information rather than as grades, and that comparisons among individual teachers and individual students are not made?

- How can the results of schoolwide assessments be used as the basis for overall discussions about students' competencies and potential, as well as to establish benchmarks for growth?

Suggestions for Professional Reading

- Calkins, Lucy; Montgomery, Kate and Donna Santman. *A Teacher's Guide to Standardized Reading Tests.* Portsmouth, NH: Heinemann, 1998.

  This guide compels teachers and administrators to be more knowledgeable about the tests they implement in their literacy programs.

The book provides an overview of tests, showing teachers and administrators how to use this information in their interaction with colleagues and students. It also provides guidelines for reading and interpreting test results, enabling teachers and administrators to create balance in their assessment program.

- Clay, Marie M. *An Observation Survey of Early Literacy Achievement.* Auckland, NZ: Heinemann Education (Reed Publishing), 1993.

This resource offers a systematic approach for observing young children who are learning to read and write. It gives teachers, administrators, education students and researchers insight on how children learn about literacy, how to carefully observe the process, and how to identify those students for whom supplementary teaching is necessary.

- Davies, Anne. *Making Classroom Assessment Work.* Merville, British Columbia: Connections Publishing, 2000.

This book provides a thorough and clear framework for teachers and administrators to reconsider how assessment is working in their classrooms. Based on current research and practice, Davies builds a foundation for student involvement in the assessment process.

- Dorn, Linda J. and Carla Soffos. *Scaffolding Young Writers: A Writers' Workshop Approach.* Portland, Maine: Stenhouse, 2001.

Dorn and Soffos present strategies for implementing a writers' workshop in the primary grades. Adopting an apprenticeship model, the authors show how explicit teaching, good models, clear demonstrations, established routines, and assisted teaching followed by independent practice are fundamental and foundational to a successful writers' workshop.

Susan Schwartz

Susan Schwartz is a principal and a college lecturer. Here she explores literacy-based school change both from her own experiences and from observing others.

Creating a Vision for Literacy

- Planning involves accepting a shared vision and having a rapport with everyone in your school, not just the teachers, but the children, the parents and the support staff. I think the relational skills are so important. Monitoring the literacy program means knowing the students, the curriculum, the teachers and the parents.

- I visited a school last week, and was reminded that I always felt that I knew my students, but I think if I had a new school, I would try to know them even better. I would know their reading levels; I would know what they are reading and writing. This school we visited had 1,100 kids in elementary, and the principal knew every single student in kindergarten and grades one, two, and three, and the different levels they had achieved according to their learning records. In my school, I knew those who were really struggling and the ones in between, but I did not know the others that well. I think today you have to do more if you want to be an effective teacher/leader.

Implementing a Literacy Initiative

- I participated in a session with a board last week called the "Walk Through Process." We walked into twenty classrooms, and, in three minutes, we could see what was going on in terms of the cognitive approaches of teachers, the participation level of the students and the instructional strategies. It trained us to really use our eyes and to look at the rooms to see what the kids were doing, to see what the teachers were doing, and be able to understand the expectations that the teachers have of kids. We could actually get an overview of what was going on in each classroom in three minutes. The whole process was an attempt to get teachers and principals to become more aware.

- As an administrator in a high school, I walked into a class and the teacher stopped me at the door and said, "What are you doing here?" I replied, "I am just here to visit. I am in classrooms all the time. I want to find out about the curriculum." But she was uncomfortable with my being there, and this meant that I had to go back to that department and ask for help. I want to be in classrooms; I want to know what is going on; but some teachers may feel that I am there to evaluate them — I know that I am there to learn. School is about creating a culture together.

Examining the Role of Leadership

- Principals are coming into the profession with less experience as teachers; they are much younger. I have had teachers promoted in their fifth or sixth year and they have little leadership experience. But, in the Principals' Course, we do try to build an overview of the issues. We teach principals to examine self first, and to really try to understand who they will be as a leader, a human being and an educator. What is their philosophy? What do they really, strongly believe in? Shelley Harwayne is a true literacy principal, and she models what she expects from teachers.

- As a principal and as a literacy coordinator, I tried to follow the same learning processes. Some literacy coordinators see their role as giving out materials. Instead, they need to talk to teachers, assess their needs, find out what's going on and help them. It's not a job where you photocopy and laminate posters. Some literacy coordinators are brand new to the role, so they need mentors.

- As a principal, I feel that I am a curriculum leader who feels strongly about my teaching. I am modeling my teaching all the time. You need a collaborative culture to enact your vision. As I walk through classrooms and notice what teachers are doing, I am taking mental notes of what is going on. From the very beginning, there is careful observation and listening to what is happening, trying to get a feel for each classroom's own culture.

- Creating a school culture is building leadership within your staff. You're developing teacher leaders. You're looking for all the opportunities to guide them into leadership, giving them those experiences that will support them. I think it's amazing how many teachers are coming into our graduate programs and saying: "I want to be a principal" or "I want to be a consultant." They see leadership as something to strive for, which I think is a good change. In my day, we didn't do that. I wouldn't have believed that I would ever be a principal. But, on the other hand, you want leaders to be excellent teachers first. There's no way you're going to be an effective principal unless you're an excellent, exemplary teacher. And especially a sharing teacher.

Managing Change

- When you are entering a school as a new principal, you need to be careful not to immediately change the way things run. Rather, you have to model what you believe. For example, I set up my office to look like a library — to look like a place where I had gathered my resources. Doing so made a statement about me. During my very first staff meeting, I talked a little bit about myself and read a children's book aloud. Even as a high school administrator, I read aloud to the staff. It was a kind of a catalyst; it would lead to discussion questions, and I would encourage teachers to share their views.

- You have to work with your school literacy team. You have to encourage and support people in order to get them to buy into your vision. I don't want to come across as an "expert." I think you can accomplish more through one-on-one conversations. For example, in my former board, I started with teacher strengths, and then moved to the areas that they themselves wanted to improve. We did a lot of collaborative planning — scheduling teacher prep time is an art! We were so fortunate to always have a program leader to work with different groups of teachers. We also freed teachers to go out and visit other classrooms. Today, you have to think creatively, but schools are finding ways to change and develop.

Conclusion

This book grew out of the need to support school leaders whose job has become even more influential and significant than ever before, with mounting achievement targets and increased curriculum responsibilities. To tackle such a complicated topic as how to lead, support and assess literacy initiatives, we were given strength from the research and practice in two important, but seemingly incommensurable fields — school change and literacy education. As Michael Fullan so aptly expressed it in the Foreword, *Literacy education, like any innovation, requires change leadership.*

In this book, we call for an acknowledgement of and respect for the multiplicity of needs of different readers and writers in different settings, as wells as for recognition of the importance of an integrated approach to change through common goals and understandings, shared leadership, and a motivation to improve the literacy standards of *all* children. We hope that the ideas in this book have offered support for the planning, implementing and assessing of your school's literacy program. Also, by reflecting on the comments of such fine educators as Carol Rolheiser, Karen Edge, Kathryn Broad, Steven Reid and Susan Schwartz, whose voices inform and illuminate our analysis, we hope that we have placed literacy theory in a practical and authentic light.

Literacy growth for all children is a powerful goal for schools to try to achieve. And, we now know that it takes everyone in the school to make this outcome a possibility. Your stewardship in this vital aspect of education is at the heart of the process — your leadership in guiding teachers and parents in developing an effective literacy progam will determine its success. We celebrate your commitment to the goal of having all children become "print powerful" as they participate in a nurturing and supportive literacy-based school.

Afterword

I have spent most of my life alongside school principals, as a student for thirteen years, (and since we moved house almost every year, I met a lot of them), as a classroom teacher in three different schools for ten years, as a language arts consultant for six years, and as a teacher educator in a faculty of education for the rest of my career. In each of these situations, I seldom felt part of a reciprocal relationship; these school leaders always seemed in a position of absolute authority, and I felt completely subservient.

As a child, I respected all of the principals that led the schools I attended, from Mr. Van Horne, who wore a fresh flower in his lapel every day, to Mr. Tilden, who allowed me to answer the school phone in his absence. But then, I was a mousy, academic child who was never sent to the office for rule infractions, and, as a result, I saw these leaders (they were all males) as solemn figureheads who seldom, if ever, entered a classroom and who were never seen teaching (or reading!).

As a young teacher, this recognition of their power status stayed with me, and I carefully maintained a distant and professional demeanor with each of the four men under whose leadership I served — Roy Howard, Ted Humphries, Roy Ito and Ivan Thompson. I respected them all. However, during those years, curriculum development appeared not to be part of their mandate, for we had several subject consultants who supported our professional development. I was a complex and sometimes difficult teacher, and these men showed great patience and faith in my efforts to learn to teach, and I was given free rein to invent my own programs. However, without the mentoring from consultants, such as the nurturing English supervisor Bill Moore, I would have wandered off in all directions, with my children lost in the literacy woods.

When I became a reading consultant, I quickly recognized the impact of the principal on the culture of the school. When you visit a hundred schools in a supporting role for teachers, your effectiveness is determined to a large degree by how you are welcomed by the school leader. What context have they established for your participation in the programs and the initiatives of their schools? What long-term goals have they developed with their staffs that involve your role as a literacy consultant? Who I could be in a school was in their hands. Where I could make a contribution depended on the framework that had been put in place, and the principal's role in the culture of the school determined our progress together. This change process has now been documented through Michael Fullan's work, and we consequently have solid grounds for establishing systems of effective school growth.

In working with schools as a teacher educator in a faculty of education, we depend on our relationships with schools for organizing our preservice students for their practicum placements, and I notice how the role of the principal has begun to change. In recent years I have met men and women leaders with deep interests in literacy learning, and many who have taken methodology courses and in-service sessions in the different aspects of helping youngsters become readers and writers. As well, in their new roles, these leaders have become aware of how school leadership needs to function if teachers are to be supported in meaningful ways toward professional growth. I now feel much more like a team member, all of us working toward the education of children.

These days I find myself working often with groups of principals and school leaders throughout North America, and I am strengthened by their anecdotes of their schoolwide successes in literacy endeavors, from achievement tests to worldwide computer network links. Together, we have learned that skill-drill is not enough; we know that children need real reasons for reading and writing in order to build a vision of what literacy can do for them in their lives, alongside those abilities required to fully participate as readers and writers. Still, in desperation from directives from headquarters or pressure groups, we sometimes find ourselves once again searching for the magic program that will ensure literacy success for every child in our school, only to realize that solid, long-range and schoolwide professional development is the appropriate answer.

My perspective of the role of school leadership has altered through the writing of this book. Jennifer Rowsell, the co-author, brought a world of wisdom to our writing sessions and to the interviews we conducted with several of the excellent literacy principals in our area. Her research and her inquiries resulted in the sharing of so much information about the role of literacy-based school change, and deepened my own understanding of the influence of school leaders in the reading and writing programs we develop for our students.

I celebrate those educators who lead from within the circle that embraces children. On a final note, I defer to Shelley Harwayne in *Going Public* on the role of teachers and administrators as models and mentors of literacy-based school change:

> *Principals, as well as teachers, can be models, in fact they 'must' be models. How can we ask students to lead literate lives if we don't? Of course, I don't take care of my own literacy because I'm trying to inspire anyone, I do it because reading and writing are two of life's pleasures. I work hard; I deserve them.*

David Booth
Ontario Institute for Studies in Education, University of Toronto

Bibliography

Adams, Marilyn et al. *Phonemic Awareness in Young Children.* Maryland: Paul H. Brookes, 1998.

Black, P. and D. Wiliam. "Assessment and Classroom Learning." *Assessment in Education,* 5 (1), 1998, 7-75.

Booth, David. *Classroom Voices: Language-Based Learning in the Elementary School.* Toronto: Harcourt Brace Canada, 1994.

_____. *Guiding the Reading Process: Techniques and Strategies for Successful Instruction in K-8 Classrooms.* Markham, ON: Pembroke Publishers, 1998.

_____, general editor. *Literacy Techniques for Building Successful Readers and Writers.* Markham, ON: Pembroke Publishers, 1996.

_____. *Reading & Writing in the Middle Years.* Markham, ON: Pembroke Publishers, 2001.

Bouchard, David with Wendy Sutton. *The Gift of Reading.* Victoria: Orca Book Publishers, 2001.

Brown, Hazel and Brian Cambourne. *Read and Retell.* Portsmouth, NH: Heinemann Publishing, 1987.

Calkins, Lucy and Lydia Bellino. *Raising Lifelong Learners: A Parent's Guide.* Reading, Massachusetts: Addison-Wesley Publishers, 1997.

Calkins, Lucy; Montgomery, Kate and Donna Santman. *A Teacher's Guide to Standardized Reading Tests. Knowledge Is Power.* Portsmouth, NH: Heinemann Publishing, 1998.

Childress, Alice. *A Hero Ain't Nothin' but a Sandwich.* Puffin, 2000.

CIERA (The Center for the Improvement of Early Reading Achievement). *An Analysis of Early Literacy Assessments Used for Instruction.* University of Michigan, 2000.

Clay, Marie M. *By Different Paths to Common Outcomes.* Portland, Maine: Stenhouse Publishers, 1998

_____. *Reading Recovery: A Guidebook for Teachers in Training.* Portsmouth, NH: Heinemann (Reed Publishing), 1993.

_____. *An Observation Survey of Early Literacy Achievement.* Auckland, NZ: Heinemann Education (Reed Publishing), 1993.

Crevola, C.A. and P.W. Hill. *Children's Literacy Success Strategy: An Overview.* Melbourne: Catholic Education Office, 1998.

_____. *Research on the Role of Reading Recovery™ as Part of a Whole-School Design Approach to Early Literacy.* Paper presented to the Second North American Leadership Academy Reading Recovery Council of North America, San Antonio, 1999.

Cummins, Jim. *Negotiating Identities: Education for Empowerment in a Diverse Society*. Second Edition. Toronto: Ontario Institute for Studies in Education, 1996.

Cunningham, Hall and Sigmon. *The Teacher's Guide to Four Blocks*. Carson-Dellosa Publishing, 1999. (http://www.wfu.edu/~cunningh/fourblocks)

Cunningham, Patricia; Moore, Sharon; Cunningham, James and David Moore. *Reading and Writing in Elementary Classrooms: Strategies and Observations*. Third Edition. New York: Longman Publishers, 1995.

Davies, Anne. *Making Classroom Assessment Work*. Merville, British Columbia: Connections Publishing, 2000.

Dorn, Linda J. and Carla Soffos. *Scaffolding Young Writers: A Writers' Workshop Approach*. Portland, Maine: Stenhouse Publishers, 2001.

Edge, Karen; Rolheiser, Carol and Michael Fullan. "Case Studies of Assessment Literacy-Driven Educational Change." Edmonton Catholic Schools, 2002.

Edge Karen; Rolheiser, Carol and Michael Fullan. "Case Studies of Literacy-Driven Educational Change: The Toronto District School Board's Early Years Literacy Project." Toronto District School Board, 2001.

Education Department of Western Australia (EDWA). *First Steps*. Portsmouth, NH: Heinemann Publishing, 1993.

Fisher, Ros; Lewis, Maureen and Bernie Davis. "Progress and Performance in National Literacy Strategy Classrooms." *Journal of Research in Reading,* 23 (1), 2000, 256-266.

Fountas, Irene and Gay Su Pinnell. *Guiding Readers and Writers Grades 3-6*. Portsmouth, NH: Heinemann Publishing, 2001.

Fullan, Michael. "Chalk Up a Victory: Canadians Have Played a Part in the Miraculous Turnaround of English Public Education. Now Let's Do Our Work at Home." *The Globe & Mail,* Tuesday, September 4, 2001, A15.

_____. *The New Meaning of Educational Change*. Third Edition. New York: Teachers College Press, 2001.

Harwayne, Shelley. *Going Public: Priorities & Practice at the Manhattan New School*. Portsmouth, NH: Heinemann Publishing, 1999.

_____. *Lifetime Guarantees: Toward Ambitious Literacy Teaching*. Portsmouth, NH: Heinemann Publishing, 2000.

Hurry, Jane. "Intervention Strategies to Support Pupils with Difficulties in Literacy During Key Stage 1. Review of Research." London: Institute of Education, University of London, 2000.

Jobe, Ron and Mary Dayton-Sakari. *Info-Kids: How to Use Nonfiction to Turn Reluctant Readers into Enthusiastic Learners*. Markham, ON: Pembroke Publishers, 2002.

_____. *Reluctant Readers: Connecting Students and Books for Successful Reading Experiences*. Markham, ON: Pembroke Publishers, 1999.

Kosnik, Clare. *Spelling in a Balanced Literacy Program.* Scarborough, ON: ITP Nelson, 1998.

Leithwood, Kenneth; Fullan, Michael and Pauline Laing. "Towards the Schools We Need: OISE/UT Researchers Offer Advice to New Premier on How to Revitalize the Education System." *The Bulletin,* 55th Year, Number 17, April 22, 2002, 20.

Lyons, Carol and Gay Su Pinnell. *Systems for Change in Literacy Education: A Guide to Professional Development.* Portsmouth, NH: Heinemann Publishing, 2001.

MacGinitie, Walter H. et al. *Gates-MacGinitie Reading Test (GMRT), Forms S & T.* Fourth Edition. Scarborough, ON: Nelson Thomson Learning, 2000.

Mascall, Blair; Fullan, Michael and Carol Rolheiser. "The Challenges of Coherence and Capacity: Case Studies on the Implementation of Early Literacy in York Region." York Region District School Board, 2002.

Mulroney, Catherine. "Testing The Unseen Curriculum." *The Toronto Star.* May 13, 2002.

Purkey, W. and J. Novak. *Inviting School Success.* Belmont, CA: Wadsworth Publishing, 1984.

Robb, Laura. *Redefining Staff Development: A Collaborative Model for Teachers and Administrators.* Portsmouth, NH: Heinemann Publishing, 2000.

Routman, Regie. *Conversations: Strategies for Teaching, Learning and Evaluating.* Portsmouth, NH: Heinemann Publishing, 2000.

Schon, D.A. *The Reflective Practitioner.* New York: Basic Books, 1983.

Schwartz, Susan and Mindy Pollishuke. *Creating the Dynamic Classroom: A Handbook for Teachers.* Toronto: Irwin Publishing, 2002.

Stead, Tony. *Is That a Fact? Teaching Nonfiction Writing K-3.* Portland, Maine: Stenhouse Publishers, 2002.

Strickland, Dorothy; Gansk, Kathy and Joanne Monroe. *Supporting Struggling Readers and Writers: Strategies for Classroom Intervention 3-6.* Portland, Maine: Stenhouse Publishers, 2002.

Success for All Foundation. 200 West Towsontown Blvd., Baltimore, MD 21204-5200 (sfainfo@successforall.net)

Trehearne, Miriam. "Balanced Literacy Programs + Early Intervention = Success for All." Calgary Board of Education, 2001.

Index

Acknowledgments

We would like to thank the following people who assisted us in developing this book:

• Michael Fullan, Dean of OISE/UT, and Carol Rolheiser, Associate Dean of OISE/UT, for their scholarship and support;

• The principals who informed our perspective, in particular Steven Reid, Susan Schwartz, Kathy Broad, Paul Shaw, Dianne Stuart and David Bouchard, for their astute and professional contributions;

• Clare Kosnik and Shelley Peterson for their friendship and scholarship;

• Larry Swartz and Andre Tremblay for their research assistance;

• Shelley Harwayne for her observations and reflections in her beautifully crafted books;

• Mary Macchiusi and Jennifer Drope, our amazing publishing/editorial team;

And, of course, Jay and Fred and Madeleine for their patience in our absences.

Credits

Article "Testing: The Unseen Curriculum" by Catherine Mulroney in *The Toronto Star*. May 13, 2002. Reprinted by permission of Catherine Mulroney.

Excerpt "Regie Routman's Suggestions for Fair Testing Practice" from *Conversations: Strategies for Teaching, Learning and Evaluating* by Regie Routman. Copyright 2000. Reprinted by permission of Heinemann, Portsmouth, NH.